STAY CALM

How a Crisis Can Strengthen Your Business

Featuring 12 Inspiring Staten Island Entrepreneurs

Prominence Publishing
www.prominencepublishing.com

Stay Calm/Mike Bloomfield. -- 1st ed.
ISBN: 978-1-988925-70-7

Contents

Introduction

By Mike Bloomfield

As Staten Island business owners, we have seen our fair share of crises and disasters in the past 20 years. September 11, 2001, hit so close to home for everyone on Staten Island. Many can name someone close to them who was lost on that day. A few years later, businesses across the Northeast were hit with the blackout of 2003. Due to a software bug, businesses across the East Coast were shuttered for nearly seven hours.

Mother Nature hasn't been too kind to us either. Hurricane Irene (2011) and Hurricane Sandy (2012) each brought destruction, the latter flooding thousands of homes and businesses just above sea level. Eight years later, we've been hit with the worst pandemic since the Spanish Flu. Commercial businesses were forced to close for many months, with nearly all still operating at well below capacity. Those businesses lucky enough to transition to a work-from-home model have had their own issues as well.

We've had consistent, devastating crises in the last twenty years. We will certainly face both old and new challenges going forward, but our past has shown that our people are not only New York Tough but Staten Island Strong as well! Staten Island Strong is our daily way of life. We don't allow ourselves to get knocked down for long. Every crisis listed above has an example of Staten Islanders rising to the occasion and becoming stronger than they were before. From the ashes of September 11th came some of the most influential Staten Island not-for-profits, the Carl Bini Memorial Foundation, and the Stephen Siller Tunnel to Towers Foundation, both of which continue to help the community two decades later. After Hurricane Sandy, there were countless everyday people across Staten Island helping in any way they could, as well as business owners, politicians, and local leaders. The current pandemic may be far from over, but individuals have consistently offered help (while practicing safe social distancing) to others over the last nine months in every way possible. Crisis after crisis, we have seen new leaders emerge to help those in need. No matter what is thrown our way, Staten Island Strong will always be a dominating factor in our lives.

In this book, you will hear from some of the most influential business owners in Staten Island. No matter what hits them, they have strived to learn from it, and have placed their businesses in a position to grow. Each chapter will tell an individual story of a crisis and a recovery. Whereas some businesses have folded after a crisis, these businesses not only recovered, but placed themselves in a position to succeed and thrive.

These stories should hit home, as many may be similar stories to crises that you have heard about in other businesses, or you yourself are currently facing. After reading this book, you should realize one thing: no matter what happens, Stay Calm and let the crisis help strengthen your business!

Mike Bloomfield

November, 2020

Finding Balance Amidst the Crisis

By Dominick Ciccarelli Jr.

I've learned that change is the only constant in business.

Our daily lives changed dramatically in March, 2020. For the first time in history in unprecedented fashion, the world was forced to shut down overnight. We were ordered to quarantine in our homes, people were dying, and on a global scale, the world had to figure out how to battle an invisible enemy. As a small business owner, this was a time of significant concern. Could my business survive or perhaps thrive in this environment? How would this global event change the course of how we operate? Could we make it?

For the last 15 years, like many business owners, I'd become addicted to work. But as with many addictions, it creeps up on you, and you're not aware of your addiction. It happens slowly over time, working every day, pushing the envelope, always looking to take things to the next level.

When you enjoy what you do for a living, it is never "work", and you want to put in the extra effort or hours to accomplish your goals. You start to skip the date nights or your child's ice hockey practice. You skip the family dinners or nights out with friends. Not because you don't want to do those things, but because as a small business owner, you don't get paid holidays off, or a pension upon retirement. Although it may appear that you earn more money than your peers who are not self-employed, when you calculate the benefits of NYC jobs you realize that in order to retire, you must work twice as hard during your earning years. As your team grows, you then take on the burden of their family members, and if your business fails, you have now prevented them from putting food on the table. Before you know it, you've created a monster that constantly needs to be fed, and will constantly redirect your attention to it, instead of the passions in which you created the business...you begin to lose focus on why you do it all.

Finding a work/life balance never came easily to me. I started my businesses before I was married, and I had no obligations to anyone but myself for the early years of my career. I could work 100 hours a week without a problem. Shortly after I got married, my wife had a career of her own and understood the work and time it took to keep a small business growing. This gave me the ability to continue to work long hours, and gave enough rope to hang myself and grow my addiction to work. Four years later my son was born, and my life changed, yet again. It was another event changing the course of life and requiring further evolution.

As a business owner, you say to yourself sometimes, "I wish I could freeze time for a moment" - not to go on vacation or to sleep, but to be able to breathe a minute and refocus. The business moves so fast trying to meet deadlines, bring in new work, keep employees happy, and collect outstanding payments. It can feel at times like a runaway train, and you need that moment to regain control. For me, this pandemic, although it caused horrific pain and suffering for so many people, did something extraordinary: it gave me a moment to freeze time. In late March and April, life was paused and that gave us that moment to reflect. The phone didn't ring, clients didn't want to meet, some employees were able to be laid off and still collect their full pay. The Monster went to sleep for a moment. A small window of opportunity presented itself, and if you were smart, you took advantage of it. We were able to take a step back, think big picture about where we were going as a team, and how best to get there. Spending time on Zoom with the team and chatting with them more informally enabled me to gather their perspectives and use that knowledge to help push the company forward. Through this period of uncertainty, rose a certain spirit of collaboration, and a desire to help the greater good.

It was unbelievable and surreal at times. I continued to go to the office every day, while my staff worked remotely. Things started happening naturally. I was able to see which employees really wanted to work to keep the office moving while working from home, and who asked to be put on unemployment so they could receive the same pay without working. Government grants eased the burden of office expenses and rent. My clients typically meet me after hours when they come home from work. They didn't want to meet in-person and I was able to have Zoom calls with them during business hours, since they were also working from home. That gave me the ability to be home early each day and spend time with my family. We started having dinner together, and quality time before bed, which would rarely occur before the pandemic. I started exercising again, biking 20+ miles a day, losing weight, and feeling healthier. I noticed I was sleeping and eating better, and I was thinking more clearly. This downtime gave me and my mind an opportunity to not think about work, and to clear my head of the stresses of the day, instead of coming home late and getting right into bed. I found the ability to think more strategically about the priorities of the business.

As an entrepreneur in the architectural and construction fields, the pandemic also presented a unique opportunity for my companies. While there was certainly a downturn in new business for a period of time, it was important that I used that time wisely to prepare for the uptick in business when it came back. We were aware that with people quarantining, much more time was being spent in the home. While of course, many people were nervous about losing their jobs or being furloughed, there was also less travel and vacation spending, so naturally we anticipated there would be a point in time when homeowners would shift their attention to their residences and desire to make improvements. Also, as people fled dense cities, new home purchases also presented opportunities for new business. There was a light of opportunity in the darkness of this pandemic. And the beauty of it was that in our work, we were helping our clients find new joy in their homes, and reconnect with their families in new ways. The business relationships we forged in this way, and at this time, are some of the strongest and most meaningful we've known.

Unlike most businesses that provide a service, we must obtain approval from the City of New York before our clients can build. Anyone who has experience working with these city agencies knows that it could be quite difficult getting to the finish line. The bureaucracy, procedures and out-of-date systems would be time consuming and inefficient to navigate. Expeditors and design professionals would spend their entire day waiting in lines, similar to the DMV, to file projects, obtain permits and get simple questions answered. I was spending 30% of my time each week in city buildings, just waiting for a ticket to be called or fighting with clerks to process documents. What was surprising was that the City was forced to change as well. They had to pivot to a work-from-home set-up. Overnight, state-of-the-art online portals were created to file documents. Over the course of just a few weeks, the expediting profession was eliminated. We no longer had to visit the Local Building Department in each borough, sitting in traffic for hours, paying for tolls and gas, spending our day waiting for tickets to be called. I can now upload documents anytime I want, 24 hours a day, seven days a week. In fact, sometimes on the weekends, clerks would respond to our requests and issue permits, whereas previously, this could only be done in-person, Monday to Friday, 8:00 am – 4:00 pm. Like flipping a switch, I gained 30% of my time back to do meaningful work, work I enjoyed doing, or to go home and spend time with my family. The late nights are no longer needed because that work can be completed during the day now. I truly believe it would have taken the City at least 10 years longer to get to this point of operations, but due to this pandemic, it fast-tracked what needed to be done, whereas before, politics or human behavior had delayed it from happening.

The pandemic taught many business owners and the government about how important it is to be nimble, to be able to evolve, and to not get too comfortable in the status quo. Anything can change at a moment's notice, whether it be a global pandemic, an economic crisis, a political event, poor health, or anything else. The businesses that will stand the test of time will be those that can evolve. We must all plan for the unexpected and be able to roll with the punches.

About the Author

Dominick Ciccarelli Jr. is a New York City-based entrepreneur with a strategic portfolio of business spanning the construction, architectural, and real estate industries.

Dominick holds an architectural degree from the New York Institute of Technology and is currently a key member at Think Design Architecture, one of the largest architectural firms in Staten Island. Think Design boasts an impressive clientele of residential, commercial and corporate work across the tri-state area. Some local work includes Angelina's Restaurante, Enoteca Maria, Crafthouse, James Carozza's Cookie Jar on Forest Avenue, and A Piece of Cake on New Dorp Lane. National brands like Family Dollar, Gamestop, Panda Express, Mr. Daymond John from Shark Tank, FUBU, and Jennifer Lopez's Viva Movil round out an expansive list of high-profile clients.

Dominick is a licensed general contractor and real estate developer in New York State. He has been building and selling homes for over 15 years. With Dominick's vast knowledge of architecture and construction and his depth of relationships throughout the industry, he has created a niche in the real estate market in Staten Island, owning and developing many projects across the north and east shores.

In late 2013, post-Hurricane Sandy, he co-founded The Construct Relief Foundation which is a 501c 3 construction-based non-profit organization dedicated to helping Staten Islanders impacted by financial, medical or other types of hardships rebuild or modify their homes.

Dominick is an active member of a number of professional and local organizations. He is an associate member of the American Institute of Architects, former President and current board member The Executive Club of Staten Island, Casa Belvedere Italian Cultural Foundation, The Staten Island Downtown Alliance, and the Salaam Club of New York.

Dominick resides on the South Shore of Staten Island with his wife and two children.

Business Awards

The SIEDC 40 under 40 Award, 2016

The King of Staten Island Award, 2016

The Salvation Army Good Samaritan Award, 2015

The City of New York, Small Business Services Certificate of Appreciation, 2013

The SIEDC Hero Awards, 2013

Organizations

Board Member, Staten Island Downtown Alliance: 2016 - Present

Board Member, Executive Club of Staten Island: 2016 - Present

Founding Member, Casa Belvedere Italian Cultural Foundation: 2014 – Present

National Association of Home Builders: 2011 – Present

The Building Industry of New York: 2011 – Present

The Salaam Club of New York: 2010 – Present

Associate Member, American Institute of Architects: 2004 – Present

Free & Accepted Masons, Great Kills Lodge #912: 2001 - Present

North Shore Business Association: 2014 – 2018

Co-Founder, & President, The Construct Relief Foundation: 2013 – 2019

Ambassador, Staten Island Economic Development Council: 2012 – 2017

Co-Founder, American Institute of Architect Students at NYIT: 2000 – 2003

Tau Kappa Epsilon – Xi Gamma Chapter: 1998 – 2003

Education

New York Institute of Technology

B.A. Architectural Technology, 5 Year Program, Extensive Architectural History Program: Italy, Spain, and Switzerland

Strength Through Adversity

By James Prendamano

In the face of crisis

Over the course of our lifetime, it is inevitable that we will face a crisis (or two) at one point or another - that's a pretty sobering fact. Those of us in the business community who are dubbed to be part of Generation X have had the dubious distinction of facing four "once-in-a-lifetime" events. We have lived through 9/11, the 2008 economic crash, Super Storm Sandy, and now of course, the coronavirus. However, how we have responded previously in the face of catastrophe, will pave the way for how we will emerge from this current crisis. Of all the possible calamities that one could face in a lifetime, I never thought I'd see a global pandemic.

When you are faced with a crisis, above all, it is critical not to get lost in the moment and remember that adversity often leads to strength. You must maintain clarity, focus, and most importantly, your spirit, especially if you are in a position of leadership. This, of course, is no easy task. Rising above a storm, while you feel like you are struggling to stay above the crashing waves, is easier said than done. If you are a business owner, your team is looking to you for leadership at this time. They will look to you not only for direction, but to see that you have maintained confidence and composure, and they will emulate your behavior. A shaky leader will only result in a shaky team. A confident and positive leader will empower and inspire others. It's much easier to maintain a positive outlook in "normal times", but to maintain that composure in the midst of a storm is a different ballgame altogether. It is in these times that our true character and strength are put to the test and revealed. I'm in the real estate business, and more than anything, I knew I had to listen to, support, and inspire my team through this time of such uncertainty and anxiety.

So, how did I go about supporting my team through yet another challenge? First, I believe it is important that you identify the crisis and analyze the situation. Next, you need to hyper-focus on the problem to uncover the silver lining. Believe me, it's always there; however, sometimes instead of just your basic digging, you must excavate. In my life and in business, I have always been the type of person who looks forward to the future and how I can be best prepared for it. There are some things, like global pandemics, however, for which you cannot plan. Regardless, you still must provide your best-educated guess regarding how long the crisis will last, who and what will be impacted, and to what degree. Once you've analyzed the crisis, it's onto the next step.

You're in the midst of a crisis, now what?

After you have analyzed your own situation, you can analyze the situation of your competitors. I find it helpful to identify your strategic advantages and disadvantages in relation to your competition, and take note of what they're doing during this critical time. Not only does this give you the time to self-reflect and see how you could improve, but it also provides you with a lens through which you can see what your competitors have tried - and what has or has not worked for them. From here, you can create a plan.

First, write it down! Once you have a plan written out, run it past trusted associates, family and friends. When you are analyzing the crisis, let history be your teacher. Educate yourself on the short, mid, and long-term impacts of crises that you've seen in the past, and trust your gut and instincts. Measure that against how you see it and what your predictions are.

How we managed coronavirus

The coronavirus certainly came in and shook up business in a way that I had never witnessed before. I had seen the crash that followed 9/11, but the market was an afterthought at that point. I couldn't even think in business terms after the tragic magnitude of that day. I was just 26 years old at the time, and I didn't think about "how I managed business after 9/11". It was more like "how did we manage as New Yorkers after 9/11?" The business was secondary to our own personal recoveries, for quite a lot of us after that infamous day.

I was in a leadership position when the housing bubble burst about a dozen years ago. Talk about scary times. Everyone was irritable and stressed to their limits. I made some mistakes during that time, yet I also made some great strides. Most importantly, what my team and I would learn from that experience was invaluable. We held on and persevered. And as we watched so many other businesses shutter, we survived. And as the market recovered, we thrived once again. Above all, the most important thing I learned at that time was "digital, digital, digital". By 2008, social media had really started to take off, led largely by Facebook and then Instagram. Twitter was a toddler at the time and was something only the young hipsters were into. I knew we had to grow at that time, and the only way to grow was digitally. We amped up our website, launched a number of digital platforms, and started delivering content. We haven't looked back since.

The coronavirus pandemic did grant us the one thing many of us commonly complain that we don't have enough of —TIME. "There aren't enough hours in the day" is a familiar adage. Funnily enough, Covid-19 necessitated that extra time for us, the "hours in the day", if you will, by streamlining and fast-tracking digital processes elsewhere. Many of us were fortunate to have extra time to spend with our loved ones, as there were no more late nights at the office, property showings, or open houses. We also saved heaps of time fighting traffic because we no longer had to suffer through our morning and evening commutes and were suddenly working from home.

In fact, time was one of the biggest challenges we had always faced as a company. I had said it for years: we were trying to fix the bike while we were pedaling it. We had no choice at the time and did it out of necessity. What this crisis actually did for us was offer us enough time to hop off that bike for a while in order to fix it - and we seized that opportunity. It gave us time to reconnect with our immediate family, re-energize, and think critically and creatively without interruption. It gave us time to figure out ways to stay connected remotely, which led to cost-saving measures. We discovered that because we had planned and made ongoing tech investments since the advent of our company, as things began decentralizing around us, we were able to keep our team centralized and connected, although not physically. But no matter, self-improvement and business growth still occurred for us. Through proper planning, when the chips were down, we were able to establish significant market dominance and take advantage of some of the opportunities. While others were struggling with infrastructure issues and trying to fix them, we were picking up market shares. People have finally recognized how critical it is to continually invest in and stay on top of digital technology.

With the extra time coronavirus afforded us, albeit via shelter-in mandates, I quickly realized that we could use that downtime to push further digitally and emerge stronger than ever when the crisis ended. We held virtual meetings and showed homes virtually, which led to actual sales. Our team enrolled in a digital marketing course and we all became certified. We amped up content across all of our social media platforms, in addition to adding informational, educational, and personal videos to our YouTube channel. We also premiered a new weekly podcast series. Here's the truth: I could not have shepherded any of this without having the utmost confidence in both my IT and digital group, and my team of tenacious sales professionals.

The principles of leadership become even more critical when you are in the midst of a crisis. I suggest you try critical thinking exercises regularly, so when a crisis does arise, you already have a loose plan in place, in which you have outlined steps to mitigate the exposure or impact on your business. In my business, we identified years ago that a digital shift was on the horizon. So, before our competition started making the investments in digital infrastructure, we began to double down, taking note of what a profound impact technology was having on so many other industries. Had we not taken the time to prepare years ago, we would not have been able to seamlessly shift to virtual offices today. Not only did this prepare us for what we faced with the pandemic, but it also gave us more freedom in the workplace on a day-to-day basis.

Preparing for the next crisis

In order to be prepared for the next crisis, you must be able to think outside the box and be amenable to rapid change. Just over twenty years ago, no one would have ever imagined people buying real estate without first having stepped foot on the property. We were still in the early days of email, and the world still largely conducted business via company phones and offices stockpiled with reams upon reams of printer paper. Remember all the faxing we did back then? The many unsuccessful attempts at faxing, all the busy signals, and failed transmissions? And that was considered "high-tech" at the time. Now, a little more than two decades later, high-tech is something completely different: it's the ability to pick up a phone or a tablet and literally have virtual access to everything I need to immediately conduct business. As a small business owner, I've always said the easiest part of the process was "starting the business". The hardest part is actually growing a business. Anyone can set up a company and put the wheels into motion, but the real challenge lies in building systems that are sustainable, renewable and cost-effective, and maintaining and upkeeping them regularly.

I have also found that surrounding yourself with the right people is key to growing a business, and having the confidence not to be the smartest person in the room is a vital component. One of the most valuable things you can ever accomplish in business is to know what you don't know. Let that sink in for a moment. We spend our lives preparing and focusing on what we do know, not what we don't. However, understanding and being able to acknowledge your areas of weakness allow you to pick the right people to fill the voids in your company.

You have to learn to be focused not solely on the crisis and the impacts it may have on your immediate business, but to be able to think along the lines of vertical integration. It opened our eyes to opportunities in other markets: the stock market, commodities market, capital markets, etc. We began deploying some of our core business practices in some of the other markets and launched Capex Funding, a white glove mortgage company. We noticed that more than ever, people were going to need professionals who not only had a profound understanding of real estate markets, which is our specialty, but they were also going to need professionals who knew how to restructure and secure debt during extraordinary times.

If you are in a position where you need to stabilize, strengthen and unlock the full potential of your real estate portfolio, you can check out our educational videos, contact the office, send us an email or give us a call.

About the Author

James Prendamano is the CEO for Casandra Properties, Inc., Staten Island's premier real-estate firm. For nearly three decades, with his trademark enthusiasm, creativity, and leadership, James has shepherded the completion of transformative projects, including major initiatives reshaping Staten Island's commercial real estate landscape.

Over his career, James has closed countless deals on residential units, mixed-use buildings, as well as retail and office leases. His expertise in project planning/design, large scale acquisition, ULURP approval consultation and retail leasing is unmatched.

His consulting clients include the biggest developers on the island, and his is the only name people use when recommending a strategic development partner.

Under his leadership, Casandra Properties, Inc., has grown from a small boutique firm to a household name. Recently, James launched the Casandra Properties Podcast as a way to offer a platform for business owners and entrepreneurs to communicate with the masses. In less than 5 months James' audience has grown exponentially, with an audience upwards of 50 countries.

James' clients include Goldman Sachs, BFC Partners, and IronState Developers. Some of his recently brokered deals include Gap, Banana Republic, Brooks Brothers, Walgreens, and Starbucks.

For the last four years, James has been named one of Staten Island's 50 most influential people by "City & State". Casandra Properties was named one of New York City's top 10 boutique real estate firms by the "Commercial Observer" and won the "Top 31 Business Award" in 2017 by the Staten Island Economic Development Corporation.

James serves as a Director of the New York City Industrial Development Agency (NYCIDA) as well as a Member of the Build NYC Resource Corporation (Build NYC). Additionally, James serves on the board of Staten Island Chamber of Commerce; as a cabinet member for the Staten

Island Economic Development Corporation and is a member of the International Council of Shopping Centers and various Real Estate Associations. He serves as on the board of directors CFLC (Central Family Life Center). James is also a recipient of the Staten Island Economic Development Corporation's 20 under 40 Leadership Award.

www.casandraproperties.com

Phone: 718.816.7799

Maintaining Your Leadership Presence Through a Crisis

By Lana Seidman

President of Help Organize My Business Inc.

"Face reality as it is,
not as it was or as you wish it to be."
-Jack Welsh, former Chairman and CEO of General
Electric

By definition, a crisis, from the Greek word *krisis*, is any event that is going to lead to an unstable and dangerous situation, affecting an individual, group, community, or whole society[1]. It is a time of intense difficulty, where we are faced with the most significant challenges. As a business owner, a crisis can be the beginning of the end, but can also be the test of your strength, resilience and true grit.

Seasoned leaders show their strength by displaying empathy, providing stability and moving the needle forward. In uncertain times, people turn to leaders for answers, security and guidance. Even if a leader doesn't have all the answers, they need

---

[1] www.lexico.com, powered by Oxford Dictionary

to be open and honest, to increase credibility and earn the trust of others. In absence of those reassuring feelings, there is uncertainty and instability.

As a business owner, you are the de facto leader of your company. Your employees consider you the expert, the one who knows how to react to an emergency and how to guide them in a challenging situation, and who financially provides the ability to support their families. When a crisis hits, all those known traits can become unknown. Your experience and expertise in matters may no longer be relevant, and that can leave some leaders in despair and their employees feeling lost.

When members of your team begin to express stress and anxiety, they are going to turn to their leader for support. Keep your words and actions aligned, and don't prematurely make promises that you may not be able to keep. How your employees perceive your leadership during times of high stress and ambiguity will define their perception of you for a long time. If you diminish or break trust, it will take considerable effort to restore it, if that is even possible.

That all sounds sensible, but there is still a challenge in maintaining your own composure and leadership presence – you are human too. Through a crisis, you are also trying to navigate through uncertainty and anxiety, and you may find yourself in an environment that is unfamiliar to you. How do you find the strength to push through and keep a positive outlook? That's easy – you just dig deeper. You tap into your leadership powers by prioritizing your own leadership journey.

Read books written by leadership experts. Listen to podcasts that inspire you or invoke innovation and ideas. In the world of virtual education, you can access executive leadership training courses that offer certifications and accreditations, which can provide additional credibility to your leadership presence. Education is power, and justifies your standing in the business world.

If you were to ask anyone to describe a leader, they may say it is someone who knows how to develop people and bring out the best in them. They may say it is someone who knows how to get things done or someone who can direct others to a successful outcome. All of those descriptions are correct, but it is so much more.

Leaders create strategies to meet their company's needs and to move it forward. They inspire others and unite them to achieve a common goal. Effective leadership is based on ideas, whether original or borrowed, that are effectively communicated to others in an effort to have them take action to provide results.

During a crisis, when you are leading through VUCA (volatile, uncertain, complex and ambiguous) times, your leadership skills are put to the test. Followers will want some sense of stability and emotional reassurance, so it is time to dig deep and follow that natural instinct that got you to where you are now.

As humans, when we perceive a threat, the amygdala in your brain releases chemicals into your body, triggering fear, anxiety and aggression. The body reacts by increasing its heart rate and breathing more quickly, and at times causing your palms to sweat. These physiological responses and sensations are designed to move us to action. Process these signs with a healthy response. Take a deep breath and pause until you can regain control and move forward in a positive direction, with the right state of mind.

For those who are regimented, a crisis can be catastrophic, taking us out of our routine, interrupting order and making us feel uncomfortable. Even the best leader can be knocked down a rung or two in an unstable environment. That can be humbling for a leader, but it can also evoke a greater sense of awareness, knowing that others may be feeling the same feelings of uncertainty, or even worse, despair.

Many successful leaders find value in keeping a journal to jot down thoughts, ideas and observations. A journal can be used to track your challenges from the day, your stresses, and on a lighter side, what you are grateful for. It can also help you revisit and analyze situations with accuracy. Journaling is a medium for reflection - one of our human superpowers. Reflection is a consideration that links current experiences to previous learnings. It draws cognitive and emotional information from several of our sensory sources, triggering us to process and evaluate data. By processing our actions through reflection, we learn from our mistakes and identify opportunities that can lead to greater development.

As leaders, a top priority is managing your own emotions, as well as being sensitive to others' emotions. So, leaders must notice, acknowledge and lean in to address their employees' fears and concerns. If you panic, those watching will sense it, thereby increasing their panic. Emotions are contagious. Modeling calm, confident behavior delivers the message that you are still capable of leading.

One of the most valuable traits of a leader is communication. There is no such thing as over-communicating, so even when you think you are communicating too much, you probably could be communicating even more. The more your team, staff and subordinates are kept in the loop, the more trust and confidence they will have in you as their leader. Even if it is bad news that has to be communicated, it can adversely impact your leadership presence, and possibly your business, if you withhold information. Be respectful to others and your employees, and communicate with them in a timely manner.

You may not have all the answers for every question or circumstance that arises, but as long as you are honest and forthright, you will not lose your power as a leader. Regular communication and check-ins should be a top priority, whether in crisis or not. When engaging your employees, be sure to consider how you are engaging them or guiding them through the difficult times. The most successful leaders leave a memorable impression, building a foundation of trust and stability for the future.

With crisis comes unchartered territory. Who would have thought we would be working five days a week from our homes, taking breaks to switch over a load of laundry, or monitoring our children's schoolwork? Who would have thought that whole countries would be shut down, or transportation systems would cease to operate? Through it all, leaders have shown their resilience and have pushed through the noise, setting clear goals and priorities for themselves and their teams.

As a leader, it is important to identify your priorities for the day. Choose three that are most important each day and be sure to accomplish at least one. Your priorities should encompass both work and personal life matters – a healthy leadership mindset includes a healthy work-life balance. Home and family priorities are deserving of their place on your list and should routinely be included.

As leaders push through difficult times, it is important to prioritize self-care. Schedule some time for breaks and utilize the time well. Take a walk outside, exercise, take a cat nap, or try some deep breathing. Check-in with friends, family and employees, and take the time to listen to them without distraction.

One of my biggest takeaways from a great leader I once knew was his ability to make me feel that the world stopped, and our conversation was his only priority. He truly listened to me and was interested in what I had to say. I'll be honest, I find it very difficult to just listen. I sometimes find myself distracted or listening to respond, or even worse, just not listening because I am not interested. But I am working on it, and I am actually finding what others have to say very interesting.

Being present and thankful, and showing gratitude when there is so much negativity surrounding you, demonstrates your thoughtfulness of others. Remind employees what you are grateful for, and encourage your team to do the same. It is important to keep your team encouraged, upbeat and optimistic. It is time to lean in and build meaningful connections. Demonstrating empathy and validating feelings is critically important to how your employees will evaluate your effectiveness and supportiveness when the crisis is over.

When it comes to maintaining your leadership presence through a crisis, it is critical to stay calm. Focus on your people and show empathy, they are the pillars who keep your business standing and are your biggest advocates, and should be your biggest priority. Communicate regularly and offer the facts - don't be quick to respond to questions if you are unsure of the right response. It is okay to say, "I'll get back to you on that" and follow up at another time. Answering a question quickly with the wrong answer just discredits your expertise.

In VUCA times, leaders need to adapt and think outside the box to conform to the current reality, while keeping their businesses afloat. Seek the advice of experts. Don't be ashamed to ask for help, or to identify new resources and opportunities. Creativity leads to success and provides your team with the platform to collaborate and innovate. Uber disrupted the taxi and cab industry, perhaps your team's new ideas can disrupt your industry.

Unfortunately, there is no doubt the future holds more uncertain times. The ability for leaders to comfort and lead their teams through those times can be the difference between a business that endures volatility and one that fails to survive.

There are a few key takeaways from my career that I believe are worth sharing.

- The things that you fear the most, but overcome, are the most rewarding.
- Focus and prioritize the things that matter most, before they are gone.
- Be agile and anticipate the blind spots around the corner.
- Prioritize self-care and make time for family.
- Mitigate risk, and seek the help of experts to take you to the next level.

- Manage your expectations - of yourself and of others.

- And lastly, take every opportunity to invest in yourself to increase your leadership presence.

"Leadership is a choice, not a position."
- Stephen Covey

About the Author

With more than two decades of operational and management experience, Lana Seidman established Help Organize My Business Inc., a New York State corporation designed to help businesses get healthy. Over the last seven years, Lana has helped business owners and their organizations establish best practices, streamline operating procedures, and gain a strong foundation as they grow their businesses. Lana utilizes her skills to help organizations set priorities and retool for a sleeker, more strategically-focused approach.

Understanding your business and how it operates is the key to its success. Is your company communicating its vision and mission effectively? Is your strategic plan still relevant? Can you clearly identify your weaknesses and effectively correct what is not working? These are the questions that require thought and care when running your business.

When hiring Lana and her company, you have engaged the services of a business coach, general manager, full-charge bookkeeper, and marketing director all in one.

Lana is the executive director of the Home Improvement Contractors of Staten Island, a non-profit trade organization whose mission is to educate homeowners on the importance of hiring reputable, licensed and insured local contractors.

Lana serves as a mentor for the Young Entrepreneurs Academy (YEA), a national program that transforms middle and high school students into confident entrepreneurs. Her philanthropic nature helped her establish the Allen Hauber Scholarship Award Program, which offers local high school seniors entering the architecture, engineering, mechanical trades and construction industries the opportunity for a scholarship award towards their continued education.

Connect with Lana:
www.helporganizemybusiness.com

Thriving in a Time of Crisis

By Sam Angiuli

Over the course of my career, I have had the privilege to work in a wide variety of industries, with all types of people and in all types of places. From finance to law, technology to hospitality, manufacturing to sales, I've been fortunate enough to see it all and learn from a multitude of great teachers and mentors.

There are many things that make these experiences different, but in many ways, most businesses share core commonalities. For this reason, we are able to shape and promote general yet powerful guidance that should help you steer any business through the most difficult of times.

In a series of guidance that I have carefully broken down into three sections, it is my pleasure to share with you, the reader, my thoughts and advice on keeping calm, surviving, and thriving during a crisis of unprecedented times.

Preparing Today for a Tumultuous Tomorrow

One of the biggest mistakes business people make is that they reactively try to cope during difficult times. Business, like most aspects of life itself, is cyclical. It is not a question of if the bad times will come, it is a question of when, meaning the best approach we have here is a proactive one. Moreover, once a crisis hits, there isn't much time to try and develop a strategy, as action will need to be taken swiftly and with meaning or it's game over. Being ready to implement a carefully thought out plan when that time does come is a necessity. Time is the most precious resource we have, and it becomes especially valuable in challenging times. Squandering it on contemplating decisions that could have been made beforehand can have detrimental effects on a company.

It is rare that crises come about in a slow-moving manner and much more likely that they will come about abruptly. In retrospect, many previous crises could have been better anticipated. In reality, they can often feel like they come about promptly and without warning. And, despite the reassuring roadmap that is laid out in this and other chapters of this book, it is an extremely unsettling feeling facing what promises to be a daunting and difficult time.

Our number one obligation in life is the well-being of our families and loved ones; for many of us, the next in line is the success of the business. Therefore, we must take every necessary measure to minimize any potential damage. Like many of us, I deeply care for the people I work with, whether they are my partners, employees, contractors, tenants, or otherwise. I am not suggesting that difficult decisions may not need to be made (quite the contrary, they most certainly will need to be made). I am, however, suggesting that we have the power to curtail these negative impacts if proper plans are strategically made in advance rather than placing ourselves in the position where we have no other option than to make a knee jerk reaction to challenges that arise.

In the normal course of our typical hustle and bustle, we frequently don't take the appropriate time to consider important factors that will come in to play later on. With that in mind, I challenge you to consider a few important concepts today. On a financial basis, do you have enough cash reserves to keep your firm afloat through a few months of negative earnings? Have you established credit history, lender relationships, and secured financing that could help you through a rainy day? In most instances, this looks like the form of a line of credit. Many businesses don't establish credit because they haven't previously needed it. This is a big mistake, as most major lenders aren't looking to form new relationships during times of crisis but rather working to ensure they are able to satisfy their existing ones. Having access to credit doesn't necessarily mean you need to utilize it or operate on an overleveraged basis; it just means it is available. Additionally, if you had to make immediate budget cuts, what would you chose to do? Not thinking about this beforehand can cause us to make bad decisions. Undercapitalization is one of the biggest challenges and impediments for a business, something we often (myself included) learn the hard way.

Let's face it: implementing change is very hard for most organizations. This sentiment holds true for both owners and employees. Think "We've always done it this way" and "If it's not broke, don't fix it" (two very dangerous concepts I might add, but I digress). You would be amazed at what people (including yourself) can do when they have no other choice. Many times, these situations put us in a corner. Necessity is the mother of invention and we should take advantage of that fact. Think of how many people were uninterested in utilizing certain technologies until they had to. Many people swore they couldn't utilize a video conference until they were all forced to work from home and quickly learned they could. This revelation actually leads to improvements because now there is no going back to old habits. New opportunities have arisen that might not have otherwise come to fruition. Embrace them.

Another thing to consider is your everyday normal behavior towards others you do business with. People will remember who you are and how you have behaved in the past. One of the earliest lessons I learned in business is: be nice to people you meet on the way up because you will see them on the way down. Aside from the fact that this is good business, it's just the right thing to do!

Relationships we form doing direct business are many times as important as those in our business network – our support group. While we work hard and are frequently in the driver's seat, I am a firm believer that nobody accomplishes anything on their own. The people around us help shape who we are and are invaluable to our overall success and happiness. Make sure you have a good support system, and equally as important, make sure you are part of someone else's!

Navigating the Crisis: Don't Operate from Fear

Another one of the biggest mistakes people make during difficult times is that they retreat from their core mission and begin to operate their business from a state of fear. It is natural during times of uncertainty to retreat into survival mode. However, there is a big difference between being calculated and cautious and letting fear and other negative emotions dictate your behavior and choices.

For this concept, it is important to keep your center! Make no mistake, many people will be depending on you, in different capacities. In order to work at peak performance, you need to invest in taking care of yourself. For different people that means different things. It could mean a healthy diet. For myself, along with the above-mentioned good habits, it means that no matter how busy I get, I ensure I make some time to play my guitar and spend time with my children. It is so easy to get sucked into working all hours, but eventually, you will be doing a disservice to those around you. You owe it to them, and yourself, to be the best version of yourself that you can be. Your business and your family will all be better for it.

It is imperative to remain resilient. Resilience is one of the most important qualities for people in our position. Too many people are counting on you to fold your cards now.

There are many factors we simply can't consider until they happen, and we will have to react and adapt accordingly. One of the companies our organization has the pleasure of currently investing in is a local brewery. When the New York State executive orders were handed down at the start of the COVID-19 crisis, our two biggest profit revenue streams vanished. We were however able to take advantage of new laws that allowed us to deliver our products directly to homes. In order to survive, we had to, virtually overnight, create a delivery business. While it might seem simple, it took a great deal of consideration and effort. Developing the smartest routes, hiring or re-utilizing employees, linking the new sales to our existing point of sales system, marketing the new concept, and forecasting demand through trial and error were just some of the obstacles we needed to overcome. Based on existing laws, home delivery was never something we thought we would have the opportunity to partake in so there was no existing plan. This is one of the examples of our quick adaptations that helped us survive. But in this instance, I digress to earlier guidance: what really drove the delivery sales and helped us survive? The truth is, it was our pre-planned creativeness and innovation in our products. We took the opportunity to proactively collaborate with other local businesses. Creating products such as a beer in collaboration with a locally beloved bakery or a hard seltzer with a locally cherished Italian ices franchise was the real winner here. People tend to have a sense of pride when it comes to their communities, and if you put out a high-quality product, and treat them well, you would be surprised at the positive results you see. Times when everyone retreats may actually be one of the best times to consider launching new products and services. It is important to remain innovative and resilient. Yes, the quick reaction to the new laws was vital for the company's survival, but the company's pre-planning and uncom- promising commitment to carrying out its core mission were what really did the trick.

You cannot freeze. Putting your head down and hoping things go away, or doing business as usual, will not work. We have our successes and we have our failures, but wishful thinking is not a strategy. Doing something is almost always better than doing nothing. There will be those who criticize, and it is our duty to drown out the noise while we keep the ship moving forward. To paraphrase a popular mustachioed president from the early 20th century, "It's not the critic who counts, the credit belongs to the person in the arena". Do what you think is right and do it in an unrelenting fashion.

Always Remember to Give Back

Our businesses and creations often become extensions of ourselves and we must remember to do everything that we can for our community and those in need, even if times are arduous for us. Whether we like it or not, it is critical that we remember we hold an important role in society and have an inherent responsibility in our communities, which means that it will always be important to give back in any way you can.

As a suit-wearing businessman during the day but a musician at heart, I would be remiss not to incorporate a musical quote. As the late, great Frank Sinatra sings in the old song Cycles, "Even when my chips are low, there's still some left for givin'". As business owners (or professionals with similar responsibilities) we need to remember that aforementioned obligation to our local communities. Contrary to the hoarding mentality, this is the time those in need require our assistance the most, and it is our duty to share the blessings we have with them.

For those who are concerned about the limits of what they are able to give, I encourage them to consider using unique methods that can take advantage of the multiplier effect. As an example, during COVID-19, the effects of the crisis were devastating on so many levels. Businesses were destroyed, jobs were lost, all of which pales in comparison to the devastation experienced by those who lost a loved one. When these horrible and unavoidable reverberations rip through our society, we can collectively feel defeated and lost. How do we combat those compounding negative effects with limited resources? Let's begin by kick-starting some exponential ripple effects of our own.

One idea of this nature that we executed was purchasing meals from local restaurants to provide to local hospitals. Think of the impact of this single gesture. This one action or one donation was able to help in myriad ways. The purchase of the food helped the struggling restaurants, the food was delivered to the hospitals helped the medical staff who were working tirelessly, which in turn helped the patients at the hospitals get the best care. It's not a very complicated idea, but the positive ripple effect that it can have in our communities is remarkable.

The same concept goes for the business community. While competition is both very real and unavoidable, the concept of "community over competition" has been popping up more and more lately. If you ask me, this theory holds a lot of water, and it's what we base much of our business dealings on. Whenever we are able to do so, let's elevate each other. In the end, we will all be better off.

All-in-all, there is no perfect handbook for dealing with a crisis, and we will never have a proverbial crystal ball that helps us see the future. But the commonalities in business make this particular roadmap a strong one. And with proper planning, commitment to our core missions, and resilient attitudes, we can not only properly mitigate risks, but potentially turn tough times into opportunities we might not have otherwise gotten.

None of the above-mentioned tasks will be easy, but if it were easy, everyone would do it. These are the times when the people we love count on us the most. These are the times we get to show the world what we are made of. Begin every day with gratitude. Attack every day with grit and purpose. Whenever you think of throwing in the towel, think back to the ancient but timeless adage: this too shall pass.

About the Author

Sam Angiuli is the Chief Operating Officer of The Angiuli Group, LLC, a privately-owned company based in New York. The Angiuli Group invests in, develops, and manages various local business and real estate ventures. The company strives to build and maintain a strong symbiotic relationship with its business partners and tenants so that it may pursue diverse and creative projects that promote positive, sustainable impacts in the communities they serve.

Before his current role, Sam worked in the Sales and Analytics department at Bloomberg LP, where he specialized in commodities and foreign exchange markets as well as economics and financial modeling. Sam is a graduate of Syracuse University where he earned a triple bachelor's degree in finance, marketing, and political science.

Sam currently lives in Staten Island with his wife Lindsay and their two children Aria and Luke. In his spare time, Sam is an avid musician who enjoys craft beer, traveling the world, and most of all, spending time with his family and friends.

The Importance of Being Prepared for a Crisis

By Stephen Molloy

The evening before Hurricane Sandy hit was like clockwork and at about 8:30 the lights went out. I called up to my wife as I looked out the dining room window, "She's here!" I took one last look outside, doing my usual rounds, locking up the house and checking on the kids before heading to bed. I was a South St Seaport electrician working for a union company based on Staten Island where I lived. At that time, I was in my twelfth year working with the company and working towards getting my master electrical license.

The morning after Sandy hit, I woke up and took a ride around the neighborhood to assess the damage and check on my work partner Aaron. Luckily enough, we were in good shape in my area. Little did we know that all of the shorelines had devastating damage. Aaron and I geared up to drive into the South St Seaport to report for work when we were hit with road closures and traffic preventing us from reaching downtown Manhattan. Not being able to get into the Seaport left me feeling uneasy. We were the in-house electricians and we feared there was damage to the electrical system due to flooding. We returned home and decided to try back later. When we finally got into the Seaport, it was such an eerie feeling. Streets were empty and dark.

We were amongst the first people to arrive with the chief engineer of the Seaport properties. His quick assessment of the damage led to our first task which was to make sure all of the switchgear and electrical equipment were turned off. That entailed us walking every inch of the property and turning off more than 500 switches in over 50 electrical rooms. Some electrical rooms were easy to open, some we had to push and pry our way through. In some of the rooms, there was a murky seawater line over our heads. Electrical equipment was covered in salty seawater. That meant there was substantial flooding and damage to all the equipment.

Two days later, the Mayor's Office sent out a letter stating that all electrical components damaged by saltwater must be removed. That meant we had a lot of work ahead of us.

People on Staten Island also needed our help. There was so much damage on the shore on Staten Island, Con Edison shut off all power to homes that were in the flooded area. Calls were coming in from homeowners needing to get their electrical system checked by a licensed electrical contractor certifying that there was no damage to their system. Seeing the devastation around the Island we knew we had to help any way we could. In the evenings we helped our community that was so badly impacted while during the day we helped restore power to the Seaport. I'm happy to say that we were able to certify and help power up 39 families at no charge. A by-product of this was that this made for future lifetime customers. Manhattan was challenging to restore with the amount of damaged equipment there was. We pulled out miles of contaminated wiring and filled containers full of electrical panels. All the while I had my flashcards with me to study for my licensing exam every break I got.

There was a company who came from out of state called Bedford; they were based out of California and they were disaster relief specialists. They had a lot of knowledge to offer on mitigating disasters. They helped us with proper protective gear, solar lanterns, and generator power. The Seaport engineers decided it would be best to relocate the electrical equipment up a level to avoid damage in another disaster. This decision created months of work for us.

The knowledge that I gained from doing the work that Hurricane Sandy created will stay with me forever. We are still seeing, in 2020, damage from Sandy. A particular building that rings a bell is on Staten Island. We received a phone call from a client that half of a residential building was without power. When we arrived on location, we were able to diagnose that the problem was corrosion damage to the main electrical wiring that was exposed to salty seawater during Sandy.

Sometimes a crisis can be a teachable moment. This particular crisis was able to help give me the knowledge and build professional relationships. Hurricanes are inevitable on the east, and being prepared for a possible crisis can prevent unnecessary devastation.

About the Author

Stephen Molloy was raised on Corbin Ave in Great Kills where he has wonderful childhood memories of all the neighborhood kids hanging out at the nearby schoolyard and playing handball, etc.

Stephen attended Wagner High School which was a little challenging because he was more of a social butterfly and not very focused on his studies, although he somehow always pulled off decent grades and was able to graduate.

It was clear to Stephen that college was not in his future, so he started searching for a career. He tried masonry and developed a great deal of respect for dump truck drivers and laborers who do that kind of work; it was a long week for Stephen, and he decided to make a move and then chose plumbing. Those who know Stephen know that dirt and water do not mix, so that was quick-lived.

Thank God Stephen was lucky enough to have a friend whose uncle owned an Electrical company on Staten Island. He was very excited about this because his older brother was an electrician and Stephen always used to get yelled at for taking apart all of his electronics growing up so he felt like this may fit.

The guys at the shop made him feel right at home and taught him the ropes. At this time, Stephen was only eighteen years old. He worked for this company for four years before his brother was able to get him into a position at a union shop which made his career shoot to the sky.

Stephen was introduced to a whole new world of electrical work and the places it can take you, from malls, live shows... the possibilities were endless, and that's when he knew he wanted to do this for the rest of his life and he wanted to become a Master Electrician.

Stephen says, "I am blessed that I have a beautiful supporting wife and four amazing children, and I am living my dream every day."

Before the Stardust Falls

By Kevin P. McKernan

In the beginning of 2020 there was normalcy as we began the year with our hopes, dreams and plans for the year. Each day, one went about the normal business of life, whether it was going to work or school, operating a business, taking care of the family, or running errands. In other words, living our lives.

Little did mankind realize that like the Martians in H. G. Wells' *War of the Worlds*, we were being observed, not by alien creatures from another world, but by a non-living virus from a cave. When it struck, the effect would be the same as the novel, a complete disruption of life.

As mankind went about the daily chores early this year, there was always something in the back of the mind about matters that should be examined, thought about and resolved. They were concerns, both personal and business. They were buried in the back of the mind only coming to the forefront late at night, right as the stardust of sleep was about to take over. The thoughts were, *"I should have some documents prepared to ensure peace of mind for myself and my family and protection for others."*

These thoughts could be about stability in life, "I have been thinking about a will and those other documents I keep being told that I should have done. I have heard about things to do to make sure things are handled properly in case something happens. I should have a better agreement, or an agreement for my business, in case something occurs."

And then, *"Yeah, I will do it tomorrow,"* and as we know, life happens the next day, and there is always something more important to do. These concerns were forgotten until the stardust came in the night. Only this time the stardust was accompanied by a vague sense that something was not right. Business was slowing for no reason, and some people seemed more tense. The money was delayed, and the traffic was lighter. There was talk about a virus that could be serious and thoughts occurred, even before stardust, *"I really should do something."* But then again, daily problems occurred and now problems with the business too, and the hope was it was temporary, that the virus wasn't serious and that it would go away. *"I need business to be normal and I will get those things done. I will call tomorrow and get it done."*

The idea of doing difficult things, the preparation of wills and other documents, is distasteful because it brings up one's mortality. It also forces one to make hard choices about the future of one's children, such as who will take care of them both in their lives, and in their property. Those thoughts bring up the fact of making sure their financial future is adequately cared for with enough money to secure their future. All of these concerns lead to an examination of the assets that are present, the insurance one has, and the beneficiaries of life insurance and other assets.

The plan for business is always difficult. There are many aspects to be examined. There is a multitude of factors involved in dealing with business succession plans. This is true whether the business is owned solely by family members, or whether it is also owned by other people. It also depends on how the business is organized: a partnership, an LLC, a corporation or some other entity. The procedures for each are different and depend on many factors. In fact, a sole proprietorship presents its own unique problems in the event of disability or death.

It is no wonder that they are put aside until stardust.

And then the NBA closed the next day within minutes; there was no college basketball, then next, no golf, and yet it was ok until then. The hairdressers and barbershops closed, and within hours, the bars and restaurants were shut by order.

In a very short time, Executive Orders were issued and then all business stopped.

It was the PAUSE.

And the fear began, "What am I to do? How could I let this happen? How could I not have been prepared? How? How?" Many were being sent to hospitals, the sirens were incessant, and people were dying. "I blew it. I blew it. I didn't prepare and I have no documents."

In the PAUSE, as businesses shut down (except for essential businesses), or were forced to furlough employees, survival was at stake. There was anxiety about personal survival, family survival and business survival. The stress of the news was such that the idea of hibernation was beginning to sound good.

That was the initial reaction, and it was understandable.

Unfortunately, this may not be the last time something like this occurs. The next time, it may not be as severe, but something may happen that will cause a disruption. A PAUSE may come again.

Therefore, the fundamental question is, how to deal with a situation like this?

Of course, the easier answer is to at least have a plan beforehand. One should have their last will and testament, health care proxy, living will and power of attorney in place and updated. One should review their insurance policies and other documents, and have them updated, if needed, and located. One should have their business plans and succession plans ratified.

So, what do you do when a PAUSE or something similar happens again?

How do you handle a situation that is unexpected, and where there are pressures from all sides: family, business partners, employees, customers, clients and the world?

To begin, I am going to borrow from another book, *The Hitchhikers Guide to the Galaxy*. DON'T PANIC and carry a towel.

Whenever a situation that is unusual occurs, there are various paths to take. One is to freeze, do nothing, let things run their course, attempt to forget about it and go into a shell. The opposite path is to try to do everything at once, even without proper legal or business advice. This generally entails the Internet and Google and leads to, in many if not most cases, unintended consequences.

So again, I say, "DON'T PANIC!" (You do not need to carry a towel.)

My advice is to take some time to relax, no matter how difficult it is, and some time to contemplate, to enjoy survival and to plan. One cannot do everything well all at once – one needs to examine what needs to be done, and take more than one step back. One needs to think about the issues, and thinking is the hardest part of life. It is frustrating to think because it is so hard, but a good plan is necessary. You have to think about what is best for the family – it can't just be put together on a whim. You have to write down the goals you are trying to achieve.

The goals can be security for oneself and family, continuity in business, or anything that one can think of in one's situation.

It is harder with business because of the dynamics, as they could involve family members and non-family members. Again, one must spend some time thinking about and writing down what one is trying to accomplish with a plan. As General Eisenhower wrote, "For every battle you must have a battle plan. Once the battle begins the plan is useless, but you must have a plan." The mastermind of D-Day was telling us that the thought process will help us accomplish our goals in the end, even though the road to them is not what one dreamed.

One cannot be so stressed that the ability to think is compromised. There needs to be focus, but real focus can only occur when one is organized both in the here and now, and for the future.

The PAUSE is also a time for relaxation. That statement may seem contradictory, but it is never truer than in a time of crisis. It is important to realize that you can, with the right professionals, get your documents and affairs in order. There will be people to assist. You are not alone.

The relaxation will help the mind. It can be physical exercise or the like, mental activities (reading a book), or anything to clear the mind.

These are also times for building and re-building relationships, even with the physical distance that is mandated. It is also a time for learning, and with the Internet, you can do it anytime and from anywhere. I have obtained years' worth of CLE credits in areas that I didn't know about.

It is also a time to see if you can do anything different in life, or even in different areas of one's business

The time of disruption can be a time when loose ends can be tied together, and a better path, or even a new path, can be embarked upon.

In conclusion, any event can be used for a positive result. The Martians of H.G. Wells were defeated by a virus. This virus, with proper thought and action, will not defeat you.

About the Author

Kevin P. McKernan is a native Staten Islander and lifelong resident. He is a graduate of the University of Notre Dame, where he received a B.A. in Government and International Relations, and a special certificate in Soviet and East European Area Studies. He then graduated from Fordham Law School, receiving a Juris Doctorate degree.

After graduation from Fordham, Mr. McKernan was employed by The New York City Council, drafting legislation and serving as counsel to various committees conducting important investigations into city agencies. He then served as the court attorney for several New York State Supreme Court justices.

Richmond County district attorney William L. Murphy then appointed Mr. McKernan as an assistant district attorney, in the capacity of bureau chief of investigation and head of the Organized Crime Task Force. After serving in that office for eight years, he left the district attorney's office as their senior trial attorney and bureau chief of the Arson Unit.

For many years, he has been in private practice with offices in New Jersey and New York. His firm, along with his counsel Vanessa Bellucci Markos, concentrates on estate planning, specifically wills, trusts and elder law matters. They represent the business in both states. Mr. McKernan is also a criminal defense attorney in all courts of New Jersey and New York, including the federal courts in both states, especially in DWI defense. He is a member of the National College of DUI Defense Attorneys, Inc.

Mr. McKernan is a member of the New Jersey State Bar Association, the New York State Bar Association, and the Richmond County Bar Association. He is also a member of the Criminal Law Section, Real Property Section, General Practice Section, Elder Law Section, and Municipal Court Committee. He is the vice president of the New Jersey State Bar Municipal Court Committee.

In his spare time, he enjoys running, playing golf, reading, and watching his Notre Dame Fighting Irish Football Team.

Tightening Bonds

How relying on foundational relationships can strengthen your business during a crisis

By James Thomson

"I have to warn you, I've heard relationships based on intense experiences never work."

— Jack Traven, Speed

It's only right that I start my chapter for the book organized by my friend (and extreme movie buff) Mike Bloomfield with a movie quote - ultimately my view will differ from that of Keanu Reeves' character from his 1994 hit, though his words relate to quite a different relationship than those I am considering here, and also relate to initiation of a relationship more than fostering those existing. Additionally, nothing involving myself and Bloomfield would ever inspire me to apply Sandra Bullock's next quote that followed the above.

I guess it's also fitting that my chapter focuses on tightening bonds, as Mike was among the group of my peers doing the best to accomplish that on a broad scale at the height of the crisis at hand, the coronavirus pandemic of 2020 (which hopefully doesn't have a dash and more years added to it). There is no doubt in my mind that the intense experiences of this crisis will tighten the bonds of many relationships had by small business owners, and by extension lead to these businesses coming out of the crisis stronger than when they entered.

As business owners, we spend much time planning for our business's next steps. However, as the saying goes, "We plan, God laughs." While the exact type, timing and impact of any unforeseeable event are not known in advance, the occurrence of these throughout the course of one's business career is a given. The most successful business owners will look back at crises as opportunities in the rearview mirror, though they may not have felt that way when facing forward; those not so fortunate (through their own actions or otherwise) are likely to forever view these as obstacles that kept them short of where they ultimately wanted to be.

> *"Every man who has accumulated a great fortune has recognized the existence of this stream of life. It consists of one's thinking process. The positive emotions of thought form the side of the stream which carries one to fortune. The negative emotions form the side which carries one down to poverty."*
> *- Napoleon Hill*

The key is to put negative feelings aside in the moment and focus on producing a positive outcome via the forces a crisis applies. As is always the case with major life events, the people around you will have a substantial impact on what your outcome ultimately is. My view as to how they did mine, is certainly one that would translate across industries.

I've spent the last fifteen years at my law firm, one as an intern, ten as an associate, and now four as a partner. Now known as Scamardella, Gervasi, Thomson & Kasegrande, P.C., the firm has been around for over sixty years, with a number of names having graced the firm's letterhead over the decades. The firm long ago established a respected presence and many strong relationships in our community, and that has remained its hallmark since before I was born. My partners and I have made it a priority to ensure that culture does not change at our firm.

There are any number of books, studies and quotes about how relationships are what drive success. Listen to any successful businessperson give a sober assessment of how they arrived where they are, and undoubtedly a big part of the story is being surrounded by the right people and the elevation they provide. As motivational speaker Jim Rohn said, "You are the average of the five people you spend the most time with." Perhaps more scientifically, as Darren Hardy writes in *The Compound Effect*, "According to research by social psychologist Dr. David McClelland of Harvard, [the people you habitually associate with] determine as much as 95 percent of your success or failure in life."

There is little doubt that having lived through COVID-19 will have a permanent effect on both the businesses and, perhaps more so, the businesspeople who survive it. So, if an event so impactful is going to hit, why not let it hit hard and in a positive manner the area that has the most impact on your business and life? Your relationships. Let's take a look at how it affected a few groups for me, and may do the same for you.

Clients and Customers

Since my first day at the firm, I have been part of the firm's real estate and business law departments. As you can imagine, my area of practice isn't the most emotional. Yes, people's feelings certainly speak to the flow of any file. But it isn't, say, divorce law or criminal law, where family matters or an individual's freedom are directly at the center of the matter at hand. The vast majority of my clients are repeat, real estate investors or small business owners. I'm in touch with most of them on a very regular basis. So, I know who likes to call, who likes to email, who likes to keep things brief, and who wants to spend more time. Time is money for businesspeople, so the majority of my client conversations are focused and stick mainly to deal points. Sure, we'll ask how each other is doing, but the longer off-topic conversations are saved for dinners or cocktails, which given our respective business and family obligations, occur much less frequently than our business-focused communications.

Thankfully, our firm's business never slowed down that much during the pandemic. So, as the Monday, March 16th workday kicked in, with the shutdown of New York City underway - a decision made when there were five reported COVID-19 deaths in the City, as opposed to the 23,000 plus tallied as of this writing - I got right to work. Yet the feeling was much different from the normal hamster wheel. Not knowing whether clients would want to focus on their file work to maintain a sense of normalcy, I allowed them to guide the direction of our conversations as the phone started to ring. But the calls weren't clients looking just to talk about how to take the next steps on a transactional destination we had already established— these calls were taking a step back, to share thoughts on what's going on, and to consider the broader impact of everything occurring. Most conversations began, and in general terms ended with, "What do you think about all this? How are you handling it?" Being a business attorney in a small community, most of my clients and contacts know each other. Many calls were about, "How's so-and-so going to manage? His business can't withstand this." People showing concern for their friends, as opposed to calling their lawyers to take the next step in a deal.

Even once COVID-19 began to set in as the new reality and the attention turned back to our files, the topic of client conversation was more often, "How do we ensure that I don't get hurt by this, while also ensuring that the other side of the transaction doesn't either?" as opposed to anything looking at simply the client's own interest. Even for my landlord and tenant clients, a notoriously adversarial area of practice where positions and ideologies are both most often directly opposed, conversations started with ensuring that no one side took the brunt of all the negative. I thought it a shame, especially on the commercial landlord-tenant side of things, when governmental regulations developed entirely against the landlord. From my view, those landlords and tenants who had done right by each other for years were working it out quite well before one received most of the cards and the other very few.

Often in these conversations, with our respective business hats off and discussing a shared disastrous event, I would see a completely different side of a person in a half-hour of talking, than had been shown in years of working together. It allowed me to greater see how the individual operates as a whole, where their concerns lie, and how they truly operate beneath the often-hardened business shell. The machinations of the normal conversation were gone, and I was talking to my clients on a more human level. The crisis had forced a different form of a conversation between myself and my clients, and by taking the opportunity to listen it grew our understanding of each other. There is no doubt that these tightened bonds will help my representation in years to come, both in understanding my clients, and in greater enjoyment in working with them after having gotten to know them better during the pandemic.

Being a lawyer, a role that lends itself to providing advice, put me in a position where I was able to be a conversational resource to my clients even beyond the normal topics that we may discuss. Perhaps, in the same way, perhaps different; perhaps in a conventional manner, and perhaps in an unforeseen creative way, many businesses provide the opportunities for their owners to be resources to customers and clients during tough times. Others being a resource for me is something I will certainly never forget, and I'd like to believe the same is felt by those I was in a position to help out.

Business Colleagues - Circle of Influence

Research shows (see, e.g., "Burnout Research" published in 2016 by Elsevier) that loneliness among small-to-medium business owners can have a significant impact on burnout. While the hours required to get such a business off the ground and keep it operating are a huge factor, being the individual responsible for making most decisions can be a lonely place as well. For that reason, it is key for a business owner to regularly be surrounded by peers sharing similar experiences.

This is perhaps never more crucial than during a crisis. While no one likes to see friends and colleagues going through tough times, it is also nice as you feel the walls collapsing around you to know that you're not alone. First, the presence of colleagues sharing thoughts and experiences can help to bring balance to a situation where individual emotions may be more erratic. Additionally, multiple minds will simply have more time to receive and process information than a single mind will. This allows analysis of the best approach to the situation at hand to develop much more quickly than if one were to take things on by oneself.

This was certainly the case for me, as I have leaned on my circle of influence heavily during the pandemic. There were many moments where I had a thought or question that required a sounding board or feedback, and a name would pop into my head as the best person to call for that. There were times where I was used in the same vein.

In particular, a business group that I'm part of, the Executive Club, played a central role in helping each other through the pandemic. The group was started six years ago by several peers in business with the intention of sharing ideas, experiences, and most of all, camaraderie. Its members have developed into wonderful resources from a business perspective, as well as good friends, many socializing and vacationing together with their families. The group has served its purpose since the day it was formed. Never has that been more evident than during the pandemic.

Initially, members shared views on what was transpiring, whether in individual phone calls, group emails, or the Zoom calls that replaced our bi-weekly meetings, allowing us not only to keep in touch, but also allowing some members the ability to work out the kinks of their first dive into video conference technology amongst friends as opposed to customers. (I'm talking about myself.) Recognizing the need to keep our small businesses present without the ability to network or project in person, a few members, in particular, saw the power of video and immediately began producing live stream shows, or video interviews, that became prominent among our local community. The group members were ever-present on these videos, having been in touch with the creators and immediately aware of the opportunity available.

Other members, whose businesses were substantially diminished or shut down, were forced to reflect on what abilities they had that may apply to other industries. Some were, for example, able to use their book of client contacts, and their trusted relationships with other businesses, to reinvent themselves as sales agents for industries that continued operations. These opportunities could hone their sales skills for their own business post-crisis, as they are now able to focus on that aspect for some time as opposed to the many aspects that an ongoing business demands of its owners. Additionally, both the new "sales agent", and the owner who gave him his shot, could have new streams of income developed for the long-term. Keeping in touch and thinking creatively among trusted colleagues allowed for both parties to seize opportunity from crisis.

If you are surrounded by the right support system, those people will *want to help you*. Many small business owners are inclined to take on as much as possible on their own and not look to others for assistance. However, the uncertainty and requirement for rapid action imposed by a crisis will all but require that you look to others more often than before. Not only will that help you solve your immediate issues, but it may also make it more natural for you to reach out for qualified assistance in the future.

And if you reach out to anyone for whom you've been present, and don't receive reciprocation, you know where you stand with them; time to weed out, addition by subtraction.

Family

"Success is not the key to happiness. Happiness is the key to success. If you love what you are doing, you will be successful."

- Albert Schweitzer

A common grievance of small business owners is that there is simply not enough time in the day. Business owners spend their careers, perhaps the majority of their lives, engaged in the conversation about developing work-life balance, and whether work-life balance is even possible. The choice daily has to be made about splitting time between work and family; all too often, the pressures and immediate demands of a business tilt the scales heavily away from home. Numerous studies have shown that failure to properly balance substantially increases stress and unhappiness, and over time decreases production. A no-win situation. Many of us are driven to achieve "success" for the benefit of our families; are we really on the path to accomplishing that if we're not spending sufficient time with those who are the focus of our dream?

As a business owner, I am tasked with not only spending the in-office time my workload calls for, but also attending a myriad of networking and charity events to maintain the relationships that are the lifeblood of our firm. As a father of three young kids, there is always more time I'd like to be spending at home. But the reality is that more to do does not add to my 24 hours each day. While my office workload actually increased as compared to last year, without the gamut of after-hours events to attend to, I had dinner with my kids more often this year than I have in the past few years combined. Additionally, without our usual hectic weekend schedule, we spent more quality time doing simple things together like going to parks and for walks. A number of colleagues who have young kids told me similar things.

Not every crisis will directly drive people to more time at home, as COVID-19 initially did. However, a crisis, whatever it may be, does have a way of driving family together. It is important to seize any elusive opportunity to start developing the balanced habits that we long strive for and strengthen the bond of the family relationships that are typically the foundation of our lives and livelihood.

Habits are tough to form, but can also be tough to break. Now in the habit of spending more quality time at home, I will be sure to be intentional in trying to keep it that way once things are "back to normal" when there is more drawing me from home, and away from "success" as described by Schweitzer.

Unfortunately, rarely do we dare to lose a moment in the rat race to take a step back to look at our approach and see if it's still the best in getting us to where we want to go. By throwing us off-course, a crisis provides a rare and undeniable opportunity to reposition, rejuvenate and recenter.

I can't wait until this pandemic is gone and its impact as an every-minute threat to many is over. However, I'm sure that some of the lessons it taught and the growth it forced will stick around for good. Going through what is hopefully a once-in-a-lifetime event with the people around me has tightened my bonds with them and reminded me why I work with and for them to begin with.

About the Author

James H. Thomson, Esq. is the partner overseeing the real estate and business law departments at Scamardella, Gervasi, Thomson & Kasegrande, P.C. Mr. Thomson has overseen these departments since 2007. In that capacity, he has handled thousands of transactions for hundreds of business owners, not-for-profits and individual clients. At the current time, his legal work is focused on the representation of commercial property owners and business owners. These services are offered in both New York and New Jersey.

In addition to his commitment to the clients of Scamardella, Gervasi, Thomson & Kasegrande, P.C., Mr. Thomson is actively involved with the Staten Island business and not-for-profit communities. He is a founding member and past president of The Executive Club of Staten Island. He is a member, and past board member, of the Staten Island Chamber of Commerce. He additionally has served on the board of directors of the West Brighton Local Development Committee. He currently serves on the advisory boards of St. Peter's Boys High School and the Carl V. Bini Foundation.

A native Staten Islander, Mr. Thomson has lived on the north shore for almost 40 years. He currently resides in Westerleigh with his wife Rilee, and three children Avery, James, and Jack.

Connect with James Thomson at www.statenlaw.com.

Producing Passionate and Positive Content During a Pandemic

By Jaclyn Tacoronte

The objective of this chapter is to discuss how a global pandemic can cause a pivot in positioning your company, your community and your purpose. The chapter will be broken into two sections: the first section will discuss the online web series, *Community Corner*, and how it provided a platform for small businesses and non-profits to discuss the challenges they experienced during COVID-19, how they have transitioned, and how colleagues were able to share resources. The second part of this chapter will go into advocacy for small businesses. Over the past two years, JMT Media advocated for Native Americans to be identified as minorities with New York City and to have an opportunity to compete for city and state contracts. After accomplishing new legislation with New York City, CEO Jaclyn Tacoronte partnered with a group of minority colleagues to create the Minority Women in Business Association of Staten Island, the first of its kind. The goal is to advocate, educate and mentor women of color and other minority women who primarily live or do business in Staten Island.

⟪

Welcome to the fun chapter. Grab a cocktail (preferably 1792 whiskey) and sit back. To understand how JMT Media was the pioneer for an online web series and how we were committed to not laying anyone off, you would have to understand the CEO, Jaclyn Tacoronte. Mrs. Tacoronte is a true Texas-born-and-bred southern gal with a thirst for smart business and marketing chops that landed her prestigious "TOP 10" advertising gigs in the world straight out of the University of Texas at San Antonio, Texas. After spending 20 years working for major for-profit entities and non-profit organizations including the Smithsonian Affiliate Snug Harbor Cultural Center & Botanical Garden, she sought to open her own firm, JMT Media. The goals were quite simple: to connect for-profit clients with the non-profit sector, to expand reach and visibility for both entities, and to expand the dynamic community of Staten Island.

The Pandemic and Pivot

Like most people, I was watching the news obsessively. The date, March 13, 2020, is one I will never forget. I had to pick up my then four-year-old son from pre-school, and I had a one-month-old daughter. I was worried about everything from airborne viruses to the normal "stay in your home for 30 days so your daughter can build her immune system". On March 13, 2020, I watched Netflix's *Pandemic* featuring Dr. Jacob Glanville. After watching the series, I reached out to Dr. Glanville with the following message: "I was intrigued by your research and your no-nonsense approach. Unfortunately, the coronavirus has reached Staten Island and I am interested in chatting with you about the virus and your research." He also had a newborn daughter, so he and I connected on multiple levels (I was an aspiring speech pathologist back in the day). With sheer curiosity, I secured Dr. Glanville as a guest on a new online series, *Community Corner*. The goal was to focus on what COVID-19 was, and how to prepare and learn more for my community. The first episode featured this pure scientific genius who had been working on an antidote for this virus. He provided hope to me. After the online web series aired, we had over 100 inquiries sent to us. I knew our community wanted answers immediately. They asked about everything from antidotes, to the basics of viruses, to protection for our families. I felt a sense of pride and responsibility to get as much information out to my community and our followers. In the past, JMT Media had managed events with over 150,000 attendees, so to distribute content in the medical field there was a sense of responsibility to get out as much information as possible from medical experts. I had never felt more of a sense of purpose than during the first two months of this pandemic. I remember working almost 16-hours daily with my newborn daughter next to me to make sure our small team of five was distributing as much information as we could.

This was the ultimate catalyst for the popular bi-weekly series featuring New York State Senator Diane Savino, New York State Assemblyman Charles Fall, Former City Council Member and President of the Grand Central Partnership Alfred Cerullo III, YouthBuild CEO Kamillah Hanks, BFC developer Joseph Ferrara, business mentor Steve Grillo, bankers, financial analysts, cultural leaders and many others. As organizations were sourcing and filtering information, JMT Media was providing real-time data and information from trusted city agencies. At one point, JMT Media had a weekly viewership of over 23,000 unique views. This information was invaluable because the team realized that now, more than ever, people were concerned and yearning for information for their small businesses and their communities. As the leading public relations and marketing firm in New York City and in Staten Island, supplying content to the masses and managing the message has always been our forte and here we were, in the middle of a pandemic, being asked by over 100 businesses almost daily where to go for loans, what to do for support, and how to apply.

This created an opportunity for us to be an industry leader, even more so to translate marketing messages digitally on social media platforms and also in "COVID-19 conscious" socially distant situations, to support a non-profit or for-profit capacity.

New York City Reboot Package

During this time, we realized several industries including restaurants, retail, small businesses, and non-profits needed a guide on the basics of digital media. So, our team created the New York City Reboot Package. In the spring of 2020, JMT Media rolled out a **FREE** comprehensive "New York Business Reboot" package to help reboot and share information with businesses amidst the COVID-19 pandemic. The packet is a six-week, step-by-step guide to help boost businesses through social media strategies, promotional material, community connection, and press outreach.

All of the FREE booklets are available for digital viewing and in downloadable formats on www.jmtmedia.nyc. To date, we have had over 630 downloads from small businesses across New York City.

Changing Laws

In 2017, my marketing and public relations agency, JMT Media, applied for a Minority Women Business Enterprise Certificate with the encouragement of Staten Island Borough Hall, Staten Island Economic Development Corporation, Staten Island Chamber of Commerce, and the Small Business Development Center. I am a proud Native American.

After nine months of an intense and vetted application process, it was truly a shock to find out my application was denied. Not because I didn't have solid financial statements and not because of a lack of business acumen; I was denied simply because of my minority status. In 2017, New York City legislation defined a "Minority Group" as only Black Americans, Asian Americans and Hispanic Americans."

In 2017, the poverty level for Native Americans was at 26%, while for the nation the poverty rate was at 14%[2]

With Native Americans having the lowest employment rate of any racial or ethnic group in the United States (Bureau of Labor Statistics, 2012), economic development and inclusion to bid and apply for city contracts are essential in creating economic growth for my borough and my city.

In the 2018 *Making the Grade Report,* the City spent more than $1.5 billion through requirements contracts in FY 2018, but M/WBEs received only $102.5 million – less than seven percent – of this spending. Of this, Hispanic American-owned businesses received just $5.4 million and African Americans received just $1 million of all spending through requirements contracts, less than one percent combined. Native Americans, zero.

With the support of Staten Island City Council member Debi Rose, SIEDC Jaclyn Taschetti, YouthBuild Staten Island CEO Kamillah Hanks, and Red Storm Dance Troupe, in December 2019, Int. 1293 was changed to include "Native Americans" as part of the term "minority".

This was an incredible piece of legislation that allowed Native Americans an opportunity to bid on city contracts. But, immediately during the COVID-19 pandemic, I along with 100 MWBEs in Staten

---

[2] https://www.census.gov/newsroom/facts-for-features/2017/aian-month.html

Island, found ourselves asking and seeking support specifically for minority women business owners.

After connecting with my colleagues, we created the first of its kind in New York City: the Minority Women in Business Association of Staten Island. The goal is to engage, support, and advise minority women by providing information, training and workshops to prepare and assist our members in obtaining MWBE certifications, government and city contacts, and capacity building techniques for existing businesses and startups.

Community is the Most Important Key

While everything was happening, even before new laws were passed, the pandemic happened, and there was always a sense of community and support. I reached out to so many people in order to navigate the new waters of uncertainty. Whether it was the brilliance Steve Grillo on the strategy side or my fearless cultural beacon colleague Aileen Fuchs, one thing is always certain, the community has many layers. So, as I am writing this chapter, I would say, find your roster of folks off whom you can bounce ideas, and if you need to change your strategy daily, weekly or monthly, it's absolutely ok. There is no set timeline for what can or can't work for you, if you try. As an entrepreneur, we continuously have to position new strategies to get the job done but during a pandemic we have to pause, pivot and produce positive content for our community.

About the Author

Jaclyn M. Tacoronte is an award-winning marketing and public relations professional with over 20 years of experience in both agency and client-side settings, serving Fortune 500 companies, including Canon, Puma, Harley-Davidson, and Proctor & Gamble. She is frequently a public relations guest speaker and panelist for New York State Council for the Arts, Staten Island Not For Profit Association, Center for Non-Profit Success, and Staten Island Partnership for Community Wellness. She is currently the CEO & President of JMT Media, LLC., a New York certified M/WBE boutique marketing, public relations, and design firm that specializes in small business marketing and the non-profit sector. Mrs. Tacoronte has spearheaded all marketing and public relations efforts for the inaugural *New York City Winter Lantern Festival* and *Winter Wonderland Staten Island Festival* garnering over 200,000 on and off-island attendees. Mrs. Tacoronte is also the Executive Producer of **JMT the BEAT**, a new online series featuring the best of Staten Island's business, entertainment, art and theatre groups (currently over 140,000 views).

Mrs. Tacoronte currently serves as 2nd Vice-Chair of the Minority Women in Business Association of Staten Island, Executive Women's Council for the Staten Island Economic Development Corporation, the Marketing Chair for Colloquy Collective, and Board Chair for Staten Island Makerspace.

PRIOR EXPERIENCE

She is the former Director of External Affairs & Business Development for Snug Harbor Cultural Center & Botanical Garden, a major New York City cultural destination located on an 83-acre campus on Staten Island where she spearheaded all marketing and public relations efforts leading to over 200 plus online and print editorials and features including the coveted Harper's Bazaar cover featuring the iconic, *New York Chinese Scholar's Garden.* Prior to that role, she served as the Marketing Director at The Young People's Chorus of New York City, where she helped position the organization to receive the 2011 National Arts & Humanities Youth Program Award administered by the President's Committee on the Arts & Humanities.

EDUCATION

Mrs. Tacoronte received a Bachelor of Arts in Communications focused on International Business and obtains a Master of Business Administration while living in San Antonio and Austin, Texas.

AWARDS

Among her professional recognitions, in 2011 she was awarded TED Electrical Magazine's Best-of-the-Best Marketing Excellence Award for Best Print Advertising Campaign. Recently, JMT Media was listed as an official 2018 Honoree for *Stars Under 40*, sponsored by Schnepps Communications. In 2019, the Staten Island Economic Development Corporation listed Jaclyn Tacoronte as a *"40 Under 40"* Honoree and a nominee for the 2019 *"Fastest Growing Small Business"*. *The 2020* U.S. Small Business Administration's (SBA), New York District Office New York Small Business Champion of the Year.

PURPOSE STATEMENT

My goal is to connect my love for small businesses and non-profits in my community.

For a free consultation, please email is at info@jmtmedia.nyc.

Website www.jmtmedia.nyc
Facebook jmtmedia.nyc
Instagram jmtmedia.nyc

The 5 Stages of Business Crisis

By John Tapinis

Weathering a massive storm, surviving a pandemic, making a bad decision, or facing client and staff issues can easily create a crisis for a business owner. Managing these situations and choosing how to face your crisis are what is most important. Being an accountant for over 25 years and a Profit First Professional (mastery designation), I have seen my share of crises/events that have ranged from terrorist attacks and pandemics where business owners have had no control, to more everyday possibilities like losing one of your biggest clients or your best employee. Despite the circumstances, what I have found is that there are five specific stages that you go through, whether you realize it or not, when dealing with a business crisis. The five stages of business crisis[3] are shock, desperation, evaluation, deliberate action, and surge burst. If you are resilient enough to reach the last stage, you will have greater success than you have had before.

---

[3] Profit First Professionals

First and foremost, no one is ever truly prepared for a business crisis, so the first stage is labeled as shock. You have just received notice that your best employee gave their two-week notice, you received a call that your biggest client is moving from you to another firm or vendor, or maybe it's the government shutting down because of a pandemic. In all of these situations you were not able to see it coming, nor were you able to stop it from happening. Your first reaction is that you are so stunned that you initially freeze up. You are unsure of what your next step should be, and it is difficult to make a decision that is best for your business if all of the facts have not been presented to you.

Second comes the terrible feeling of desperation. You are still at a point where you are unable to make a decision, but repercussions from the event that took place are already having an effect on your business. Most business owners, in a desperate attempt, start to make decisions that are generally not in the best overall interest of the business, but are seen as short-term fixes that in essence could hurt the business in the long run. In this stage you are thinking of cash flow - specifically cash outflow, how to minimize the cash going out by canceling subscriptions both in business and personal, negotiating with debtors, etc. On the cash inflows, you ask clients who have a balance due, "What can you afford?" to help you make ends meet.

The third stage is evaluation, which makes the business owner think about and analyze what is truly at stake, and the direction in which he or she needs to move. There are two distinct points at this stage where you might find yourself: you might be at the bottom of the bell curve, stuck in a stagnate position, still not knowing what your next move should be, or you feel that you have all of the facts and information you need to move into consideration and start making decisions. There is a possibility that wrong decisions will be made at this stage, but wrong decisions at this stage are generally less detrimental to the business because information was used to make the decision. Evaluation of debt is also a factor at this stage, which means there needs to be a decision as to whether or not you choose to obtain new debt to survive. It has always been my advice to use extreme caution when making this decision, because it is very easy to find yourself in a position where you have saddled yourself with debt payments for the foreseeable future.

Deliberate action is the fourth stage of a business crisis, and this is where you might find yourself making positive progress. After all that you have been through you may not realize it, but this is where things start to get better. You have been able to formulate a clear picture of your surroundings and you have gathered enough facts and information that you are confident in the decisions you are making. As a result of these well-thought-out decisions and all of the planning that has taken place, it becomes evident that the company begins to rebound. You gain confidence and realize that the event that caused your business crisis will not define you, but make you stronger and a better businessperson at that. The "light at the end of the tunnel" is what continues to motivate you and travel even a few steps further.

Last but not least is the stage known as surge burst. You have made decisions, committed to what you feel are the best next steps to move forward and now you are seeing that your business is stabilizing. Things are definitely better, but we also realize that things are certainly not the same. What you take away from it all, is that you have found a way to adapt to the situation you were forced to face. Although stressful, this has prepared you to deal with any form of crisis your business might face, whether it be complex or simple. You have been given the tools to create business opportunities as you look to grow and move forward past the crisis.

The five stages of business crisis help to prepare you mentally and organize your thoughts when approaching a crisis. A common thread throughout all of the stages is seeking the best guidance to make well-informed decisions. Accounting professionals are an excellent resource to help you work through business issues, as your accountant knows many of the key details about your business. An accountant is able to aid you in your decisions and help you prepare for and execute what needs to be done to save a business that is facing a crisis. Most importantly, your business is your livelihood. You should always utilize your resources, so as to not look back at decisions you made and wonder if they really were the best ones to make. Whether you look back and say your business suffered a crisis during Superstorm Sandy, the Covid-19 pandemic, or because of the loss of your biggest client or top employee, no matter what the situation was, following the five stages and seeking advice is my best advice!

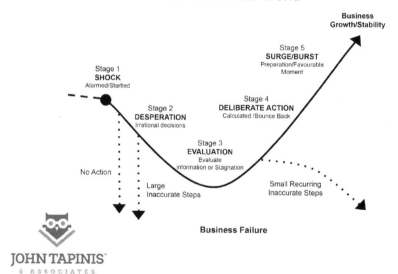

The Business Crisis Trend

About the Author

John Tapinis, the founder of JTA, is a native Staten Islander who started his business in 2002. He enjoys volunteering his time with various organizations; he was the chair of the board of the Staten Island Mental Health Society for over seven years, and is currently a Richmond University Medical Center Hospital board member. He has a passion for, and has devoted his career to, helping people, their families and their businesses.

Before starting JTA, John received his BS in Accounting from The College of Staten Island. He began working at Ernst & Young LLP and earned his EA license from the Internal Revenue Service. In January 2002, he decided to open his own firm. He possesses a great deal of expertise in many aspects of the tax and accounting world as it pertains to individual taxes, corporate taxes, partnerships, bookkeeping, payroll, exempt organizations and trusts. He continuously educates himself in these fields to best help his clients.

John is an owner and is on the board of the Italian soccer team Venezia FC in Venice Italy since October 2015.

John lives in New Jersey with his wife, Jennifer, and two wonderful sons, Nicholas and Anthony. He is a devoted family man and enjoys attending his kids' sporting events, and traveling. He will gladly take any opportunity to book a trip and explore new places with his family.

How We Became Staten Island's Covid Testing Lab

By Sadia Malik

InterScience Diagnostic Lab, located in the Great Kills section of Staten Island, has long been at the forefront of cutting-edge medical diagnostic since it was founded by Dr. Mazhar Malik in 1980. Initially, a full-service clinical lab, it was transformed into a specialty lab in 2001 focusing on anatomical and molecular diagnostic and treatments for cancer, including gastroenterology, hematology, gynecology, urology, and dermatology.

More recently, it has become a leader in the field of genomics: the mapping of DNA and RNA. This has been immensely successful in tracing inherent cancers as well as the causes of neurological conditions such as Autism, Batten disease, Alzheimer's, Down syndrome, and Fragile X Syndrome.

In 2020, InterScience Diagnostic Lab (ISDL) faced a new challenge in the face of the worldwide COVID-19 pandemic; the disease, known officially as SARS-COV-2, has affected over 250,000 New Yorkers alone and killed nearly 24,000 to date. It was affecting the respiratory system and also the gastroenterology system primarily those in advanced age groups, usually with underlying conditions such as diabetes and heart disease. However, the disease has proven to be somewhat unpredictable, as even relatively younger, healthier carriers have been incapacitated or even died from the condition. As the pressure and panic were setting in, the staff and leadership at InterScience were determined with a clear goal in mind: testing, testing, testing.

Without proper testing available on Staten Island, the ISDL transitioned into the small borough's only COVID testing lab, guided by Dr. Malik and his daughters, Sadia and Sarah. Since March, the highly trained staff has conducted over 25,500 tests with no co-pays or extra charges, regardless of insurance status. Despite the risks involved, staff members have been working non-stop while taking the proper precautions and providing the best care possible to those affected. As demands for testing became critical within the nursing home employees and staff, another organized effort was now made to test and provide results within 24-48 hours. With the IT infrastructure in place, compliance officers geared up, couriers and staff ready, and directors in molecular genomics eager, the goal was achieved in recording breaking time. This would have not been possible without the leadership of the lab's founders and staff. New York State Department of Health and Federal agencies have been very supportive to guide our lab with the requirements during the pandemic. Local and State officials offered their resources effectively, putting politics aside. Communities and cultural organizations helped pull together to support the endeavor of an unknown Covid 19 and its complexities.

About the Author

Sadia Malik Sheikh is a first-generation Muslim American-Pakistani, born in Staten Island. She received her high school Degree from Notre Dame Academy and her degree in health care administration from St. John's University. Her medical background includes Staten Island university hospital and Staten Island physicians' practice. For the last 25 years, she is Vice President of operations and network for Interscience.

Since Sadia is a bilingual Urdu and English-speaking professional, she has helped to bridge her community needs with the local, state, and federal agencies. Sadia is on the executive committee of the Staten Island Democratic Party. She has volunteered hundreds of hours in assisting indigent patients and families with medical and social service requirements for many years.

She has worked on the board of the Pakistan Civic Association of Staten Island for over 20 and years has tried to bridge her community struggles on a local and state basis.

Her involvement with small businesses on Staten Island has helped with many job placements and mentoring programs for her community and many starting out medical professionals. She has always been the voice to the many Muslim and Pakistani Americans across the country. She has held many volunteer board positions to better serve her cultural and medical community in the years.

Sadia has been actively involved with the Muslim Observer Newspaper (TMO) a weekly newspaper, founded in 1998, focusing on issues relevant to Muslims and Islam. It is based in Farmington, Michigan, United States – a publication by the parent media organization Muslim Media Network Inc.[1] It reaches all 50 United States and its website, muslimobserver.com, is visited by thousands of people every day. The newspaper has a circulation of 20,000. The Muslim Observer (printed newspaper) is mostly distributed free of charge to the mosques and cultural centers in the community. It has national and international correspondents and publishes a wide variety of departments for its readers, including a children's section, a health and nutrition section, and various regional pages, including the ones for Houston, southeast Michigan, and south Florida.

Her most recent work has been recognizing the special needs of Muslim detainees in immigration custody and detention facility to ensure the basic Islamic tools are readily accessible such as halal meals, prayer Rugs, lady's hijab, Islamic lectures, and English translated Qurans.

Sadia has held a board position with the Salvation Army of Staten Island, a non-for-profit organization. She has served as the chairman of the Staten Island democratic gala in the past years.

In her meeting with Vice-President Biden in 2016, Sadia stressed her community's needs to the White House, particularly the needs of professional mentors for the community and small business struggles and needs.

Sadia along with her relations with the District Attorney of Staten Island has helped and assisted many battered and abused women within her community through her involvement with the local mosque and churches. Her outreach has further helped these families maintain jobs and provide better lives for young children. Sadia has successfully maintained her liaisons and network because of her friendly and loving approach to helping the community. She never says no and always tries her best to find a solution to a problem. She has been labeled as a "crisis manager" among her peers because of her ability to understand and bridge the community and people's problems with governmental solutions. Her relentless desire to help others is seen with the outstanding number of supporters she has within the community of Staten Island.

She is currently on the board of the Pakistani Staten Island Civic Association.

Sadia is on the board of trustees for the Islamic Society of Staten Island

Sadia is on the honoree board of East/West University in Illinois.

Sadia is an active member of the Brooklyn Islamic Center based in Bayridge, Brooklyn.

Sadia is the oldest daughter of Dr. Mazhar and Shahnaz Malik. An immigrant professional family that has been established in Staten Island for over 50 years.

She has two younger sisters, Rabia and Sarah that support her in all her social and professional endeavors. It is at her roots within her family that she has learned the values of eastern and western cultures and ethics. Sadia is married to Ahsan Sheik and has two lovely sons, Fahad and Yousuf. She continues to instill the values and cultures of her background in her family by involving her children in much of her charity work as the second generation of American Muslim Pakistani living in Staten Island and through the New York City.

Lights, Camera, Covid

By Todd Bivona
and Michael Graziuso

There are lies.

There are damn lies.

Then there's 'production paperwork'.

Simply put, the best-laid plans in television and film productions can go out the window once the cameras roll.

Experienced directors, producers, and crew members know that staying on schedule can be challenging. There are many variables in our unique industry that can hamper even the most skilled professionals. Broadcasts and recordings outside, for instance, place the crew and valuable equipment against the elements. Being on location and not in the friendly confines of a studio opens up a slew of potential issues.

No matter the circumstance of oddities that can be presented on set - in a studio or on location - the job gets done. If the obstacles are too great to overcome, modifications to script or the storyboard are adjusted accordingly and a new plan is drawn up to, "make it work." The saying, "we fooled them again" is often said out loud when the team manages to get the job done; we did it darn well and the end result is a product that many find to be a complex technical feat, when in reality, we are all just professionals, going about our duties as normal. In this industry, however, as creative, dynamic, and changing it is, adapting to the times and situations is what we are all about so for us, it's nothing new or difficult. Yet, when we completed the task, we jokingly say... we fooled them...again.

"It takes a village" is another common phrase in productions and with good reason: it takes many people to make a shoot happen, days, weeks, months prior, day of, and then the post-production team gets its hands on it. The point here is that any good show or movie or recording will be executed but it takes the right team, the right chemistry, the right synergy, in order to put out a solid product. When the stakes are raised and the problems arise, you rely on your support group - the crew - to get things done and be flexible with working under such developing situations.

For many small and large companies throughout the world - including Gotham Trinity Productions - there were great plans for the year 2020. Generally speaking, there was much optimism surrounding the year: many felt the start of a new decade was a time to be reborn or start new or prepare for another technological and financial surge.

Unfortunately for all of us, a global health crisis upended our lives and changed the trajectory of our personal and professional lives, forever. Like many businesses, Gotham Trinity was negatively impacted by the COVID-19 global pandemic... initially. The postponement or cancelation of live sports and entertainment events had severe, negative financial implications. In addition, Gotham Trinity had a premiere planned for the pilot episode for a proof of concept TV series that was to take place in New York City, viewed by key representatives in the television and film industry.

As we know, when people started working from home, the importance of being able to connect with clients and colleagues became significant. The lack of in-person gatherings, however, pushed the importance of video content creating to the forefront. Whether it was basic meetings, conferences, summits, or producing virtual events, small and large businesses felt the need to adapt.

Many companies came to us, seeking our guidance and suddenly, our services were very much in demand. We executed a new approach to what we do and assisted businesses with the following:

- Live broadcasts - Facebook, YouTube, Instagram, etc. sometimes, included an in-person presence, plus remote guests...or, done completely with guests from their home or office.

- Testimonials - a perfect time to get people while they are stuck at home, providing great words about how they utilized "x" business in the past.

- Leadership Summit - raising funds for local non-profits, discussing leadership through a crisis.

- Telethon - pre-recorded performances along with local celebrity appearances for local theatre.

- "Music video" edits - submitted videos from participants at a non-profit, edited together to show them singing a song.

- Promotional videos for non-profits

One of the highlights was hosting and producing a segment for Staten Island's daily newspaper and their digital presence, SILive.com, "#TogetherSI Business Spotlight," shedding light on the local business community, sharing their general story and how they battled COVID. We also produced a 15-minute show before a NEW Drive-In Movie Theater.

We adapted.

We made ourselves necessary and kept ourselves relevant.

Short and long-term plans of ours that were not supposed to start for a year or two had their timelines pushed up because of COVID. The idea of LIVE shows, broadcasting, promotional pieces, commercials for businesses to show they are still open, and general consistent programming... all pushed up on our timeline because there was a need to fill a void.

There is an abundant need for video content to be produced on a professional level without being outrageously priced, focusing on the small business community that needs the attention now, more than ever. With in-person communication and group gatherings limited or non-existent in some aspects of life, reliance on video has reached new heights. Being able to convey a message through a video camera has been of utmost importance for many people, brands and services.

About the Authors

Todd Bivona

Born in Bogota, Colombia in South America, Todd Bivona was adopted at three months old by the Bivona family, based in Canarsie, Brooklyn. Todd lived there until he was eight and moved to Tottenville in Staten Island, New York and resided there for 25 years with a four year stop at Marist College in Poughkeepsie, New York. There, he earned a Bachelor of Arts Degree, concentrated in Sports Communication.

In addition to continuing his track career at Marist – which began at Tottenville High School - he was involved in the campus television network, Marist College Television, where he gained experience working in live and taped programming for sports, news and entertainment. This is where he realized TV broadcasting and film was for him.

STAY CALM | 119

As a junior at Marist, Todd interned at HBO Sports, working on set as a production assistant for "Inside The NFL," "Real Sports with Bryant Gumbel" and various boxing events in the tri-state area. From there he bounced around from gig to gig, network to network, primarily as a production assistant, jib technician, camera utility and eventually moving up to a stage manager which is what he still does now at MLB Network, NBC Sports, ESPN, FOX Sports or whoever calls.

The most enjoyable work experience for Todd has been his involvement in 4 of the last 5 Olympics, working as a digital producer in 2010 for the Vancouver games – based in Stamford, Connecticut – on site for Sochi 2014, Rio 2016 and the 2018 Olympics in South Korea.

Gotham Trinity Productions was a dream that began after his stint as a sports reporter in 2008 and realizing the power in and necessity for local event coverage, specifically, sports and other bigger happenings. Having been official for three years and functioning for five, GTP has evolved from a short film focused group, to a live multi-camera broadcasting, commercial, promotional video producing company that is looking to take the approach network TV has on a national scale and downsize it to fit the needs of the local community.

Michael Graziuso

Born in Brooklyn, Michael Graziuso was always surrounded by the film culture. As a child, it was his family's video store business that allowed him access to view a plethora of cinematic classics. When films were shooting in his neighborhood he would sneak on set and have to employ some smooth talking to get himself out of trouble. The crew usually took a liking to him, giving him small tasks and all the while he would observe the controlled chaos.

As he was developing his own style of filmmaking his family moved to Staten Island and he was no longer able to simply hop over to the family business and head to sets. This left a void in his heart.

He pursued the family business and contributed to its successful growth by obtaining relevant licenses and certifications, one of which required college credits. He chose to attend Full Sail University where he obtained his Bachelor's Degree of Science in Film and graduated as the Valedictorian of his class. He soon realized that he was not going to wait for someone to hire him; he would just hire himself.

Gotham Trinity has given him the opportunity to produce, write and direct multiple short films, documentaries, live events and commercials.

Now, Michael is a producer and entrepreneur with several successful businesses. He is fortunate to work every day with his best friends and living his dream.

Wise wisdom from Master Yoda: "Do or Do Not, there is no try."

Down but Never Out:
Surviving Back-to-Back Ransomware Attacks

By Mike Bloomfield

When you learn about cyber-attacks on the mainstream news, it's because the attack was large enough to warrant a nationwide or worldwide response. Whether it's against big businesses (Target breach in 2013[4] or Capital One in 2019[5]) or public institutions (Baltimore in 2019[6] or 22 Texan towns in 2019[7]), these attacks can put millions of people's private information at risk. These attacks capture the public consciousness because of this reason. However, once the fallout settles and the

---

[4] McCoy, Kevin. "Target to Pay $18.5M for 2013 Data Breach That Affected 41 Million Consumers." *USA Today*, Gannett Satellite Information Network, 23 May 2017, www.usatoday.com/story/money/2017/05/23/target-pay-185m-2013-data-breach-affected-consumers/102063932/.

[5] "Information on the Capital One Cyber Incident." *2019 Capital One Cyber Incident | What Happened | Capital One*, 23 Sept. 2019, www.capitalone.com/facts2019/.

[6] Duncan, Ian, and Colin Campbell. "Baltimore City Government Computer Network Hit by Ransomware Attack." *Baltimoresun.com*, Baltimore Sun, 30 June 2019, www.baltimoresun.com/politics/bs-md-ci-it-outage-20190507-story.html.

[7] Allyn, Bobby. "22 Texas Towns Hit With Ransomware Attack In 'New Front' Of Cyberassault." *NPR*, NPR, 20 Aug. 2019, www.npr.org/2019/08/20/752695554/23-texas-towns-hit-with-ransomware-attack-in-new-front-of-cyberassault.

entity starts its recovery from the attack, the story is forgotten, and the public moves on to the next news cycle.

The essential problem with the media reporting of cyber-attacks is that the public begins to believe that cybercriminals are only focusing on the targets with the largest wallets- the big guys. If cybercriminals are smart enough to crack the security of a multi-million-dollar entity, why would they waste their time with smaller targets, such as the local accountant or lawyer? This tends to be the idea many small business owners want to lead themselves to believe. While it is true that the most proficient cybercriminals will go after those with the best defenses, the reality of the situation is that most cybercriminals aren't the elite hackers you see in movies or on the FBI's Most Wanted list. To propose an alternative perspective, if you were an up-and-coming criminal, would you rather rob from the deli or the bank across the street? If your answer is the bank, odds are you aren't as good as you think you are, and you'll end up in the slammer in no time. Banks have dozens of security cameras, a silent alarm, bulletproof glass, traceable bills, and possibly a security guard. Although the haul you'd receive from the bank is much greater than the deli, the challenges and risks you'd face are much greater as well. A deli's physical security is nowhere near that of a bank's, and your odds of getting away, even though it's a smaller haul, are much greater. If you're successful, you can expand your skills to other delis, and maybe one day you'll have the same amount of money as one bank robbery.

Now let's equate this scenario to cybersecurity. The best hackers can breach governments and big businesses and receive a massive payday; however, even the smallest mistake can lead to their arrests. The stronger security measures (dedicated IT staff, business-grade firewalls, data backups) in place for these large entities are also a barrier to entry to those less skilled (and more numerous) hackers. Whereas governments and big businesses are the banks in the previous scenario, small businesses are the delis. The less skilled cybercriminals, which are the vast majority, target small to medium businesses (SMBs) because they know SMBs have a fraction, if any, security measures in place to stop them. One of the most effective tools a cybercriminal utilizes is ransomware. The FBI offers the best overview of ransomware:

Ransomware is a type of malicious software, or malware, that prevents you from accessing your computer files, systems, or networks and demands you pay a ransom for their return. Ransomware attacks can cause costly disruptions to operations and the loss of critical information and data.

You can unknowingly download ransomware onto a computer by opening an email attachment, clicking an ad, following a link, or even visiting a website that's embedded with malware.

Once the code is loaded on a computer, it will block access to the computer itself or data and files stored there. More menacing versions can encrypt files and folders on local drives, attached drives, and even networked computers.

Most of the time, you don't know your computer has been infected. You usually discover it when you can no longer access your data, or you see computer messages letting you know about the attack and demanding ransom payments.[8]

As of August 2020, the average ransomware payment was $111,605.[9] Ransomware demands aren't static however, and can increase as the deadline for payment draws near. While cybercriminals who target SMBs aren't as sophisticated as those who hack governments, they're not stupid. Payments are almost always demanded in Bitcoin, which is an untraceable digital currency and not easy to obtain on short notice. If paying the ransom is your only option, which the FBI highly discourages (we don't negotiate with terrorists), the demand may increase, or your files may be deleted as you're scrambling to obtain the currency. There is also a chance that, even if you pay the ransom, your files will not be decrypted or the ransomware code will reside on your computer to strike at a later time (if you paid once, odds are you'll pay again!).

---

[8] "Ransomware." *FBI*, FBI, 3 Apr. 2020, www.fbi.gov/scams-and-safety/common-scams-and-crimes/ransomware.
[9] "The Cost of Ransomware Attacks." *Nationwide*, Aug. 2020, www.nationwide.com/cps/cic/blog/cost-of-ransomware-attacks.html.

Ransomware and other cyber-attacks are a reality of conducting business in the information age. Unprotected SMBs are the most vulnerable and can suffer cascading losses not limited to the attack and recovery itself. Loss or theft of private customer information can severely damage customer relations, followed by wider public relations damages (each state in the U.S. has its own laws and protocols regarding a breach, but all require you to notify customers in some capacity if your business suffers a breach). Business partnerships can be jeopardized if intellectual property is stolen. Because of this, some larger businesses are now requiring proof of sufficient cybersecurity within potential SMB partners. Big businesses not only have the capital to protect themselves from ransomware but if they do fall victim, they also have the funds to cover all aspects of the recovery. SMBs, for the most part, don't have that luxury.

It's important for SMBs to understand that cyber threats, such as ransomware, are a reality of the times and will continue to evolve. The clock is ticking for SMBs who refuse to implement cybersecurity policies for any reason. It's not about "if" you'll be breached, but "when."

When an SMB looks for help with cybersecurity, it's important to understand the difference between the break-fix model and managed services. Break-fix has been around since computers have been utilized in the workplace. The IT person helps when an issue arises and that help ends when it's resolved. Break-fix is still utilized today, however, it's woefully insufficient given the complexity of the cyber-attacks that can occur. Ransomware, if a public decryption key isn't available, has no possible remediation under the break-fix model. You can't simply 'brute-force' decrypt your files. Managed services, however, offer solutions and processes to recover from most cyber-attacks. Whereas break-fix is a reactionary solution, managed services are a proactive solution. Instead of calling the IT help desk for every computer issue, managed services providers (MSPs) continuously monitor your computers and remediate problems before they arise. The job of the MSP is to not only monitor for the day-to-day computer issues an SMB faces but also to protect from cyber-attacks. This protection includes business-grade routers/firewalls, cybersecurity training for employees, proactive antivirus that monitors for possible cyberattacks before they take root, and, most importantly, setting up a routine and encrypted backup alongside a disaster recovery plan. If ransomware were to penetrate these defenses and take hold of your SMB, the MSP would boot the latest data backup. Booting from the latest backup that isn't infected with ransomware is the easiest solution, however, many SMBs either have outdated backups, unencrypted backups, or no backup solution whatsoever.

If the last paragraph is overwhelming, let's use a real-life example of how crucial not only data backups are, but a complete cybersecurity suite as well. While Tekie Geek highly recommends that older clients migrate to a complete cybersecurity solution, some clients have remained on the business continuity and disaster recovery plan. (BCDR - a set of processes and techniques used to help an organization recover from a disaster and continue or resume routine business operations).[10] This particular SMB had an "IT guy" before Tekie Geek and believed that he had properly protected their business, which is why Tekie Geek only handled their BCDR. Given the lack of continuous monitoring of their network, a ransomware attack occurred after an employee clicked a link on a suspicious email. After the initial shock and panic by the SMB, Tekie Geek was able to recover from the latest backup (under Tekie Geek, encrypted backups occur as often as every five minutes). After recommending an IT security audit, which would identify security flaws in their network, the SMB refused. The ransomware was gone, why should they worry? Well, a few days later, the ransomware returned and encrypted all their files. It had resided on a computer and stuck again. After repeating the recovery process a second time, the SMB agreed to undergo a security audit. After the audit was completed and the findings were compiled , the results clearly showed how the SMB was completely vulnerable. The audit showed thirty

---

[10] "What Is Business Continuity and Disaster Recovery (BCDR)? - Definition from Techopedia." *Techopedia.com*, 17 Jan. 2017, www.techopedia.com/definition/13767/business-continuity-and-disaster-recovery-bcdr.

users having local administrative rights. This means that everyone in the SMB could access every file, regardless of job roles. This is how the ransomware was able to infect every file. If administrative rights were properly distributed, and, for example, a secretary fell for a ransomware link, only the files he/she had access to would be affected. While certainly not ideal, it's a better scenario than having the entire business infected. Another find was the lack of endpoint protection (endpoint meaning the computers used by employees). On top of the administrative holes, the lack of proactive antivirus on these endpoints allowed the ransomware to spread across the network. Finally, a lack of employee training in identifying phishing emails and suspicious links is the reason why the ransomware was able to enter the network. In most cases, ransomware is only able to infect networks if an employee clicks on a suspicious email link, advertisement, or website. Employee training is included in most MSP packages, including Tekie Geek's. After discussing the results with the SMB, they decided to transition to full managed services.

The SMB is now properly equipped to handle any future IT crises. Facing a ransomware attack is a traumatic experience for any business owner, let alone two attacks in one week. While MSPs preach about the dangers associated with lax cybersecurity within SMBs, some business owners may not truly believe these threats exist until they experience them firsthand. The dangers are not limited to ransomware, however. The theft of customer information, malware, and brute-force attacks can also lead to significant, costly downtime for a business. The job of the MSP is to not only protect against these cyber-attacks but any technology-related downtime. Staten Islanders remember the devastation that Superstorm Sandy caused to our infrastructure. Natural disasters (hurricanes, fires, nuclear winters, etc.) are infrequent but cause significantly longer downtime. SMBs unprepared for threats, both natural and unnatural, are playing a dangerous game against time (to quantify how downtime can cripple your business, visit downtime.tekie geek.com to use our Downtime Calculator; costs are broken down from hour to day to week). The example SMB learned firsthand the chaos of a double ransomware attack and decided to invest in a cybersecurity plan that protects them from all angles. Should a threat break through the defenses, they also have the tools and plans in place to recover with minimal downtime.

The internet, and more specifically conducting business on the internet, can be compared to the Wild West. Just like how criminals could rob a train and escape on horseback, cybercriminals can rob your business and get away without a trace. Falling victim to a ransomware attack not only hits you when you pay the ransom, but could also fatally wound your public relations, customer trust, and business partnerships. The example SMB was lucky that they, at the very least, had a competent

Business Continuity Disaster Recovery Plan in place that allowed them to recover from two ransomware attacks in one week, but so many others aren't as lucky. SMBs account for 43% of all cyber-attacks,[11] and given that ransomware attacks are on the rise (350% increase from 2017 to 2018),[12] there's no reason to believe that things will get better anytime soon. While the news focuses on the big breaches, SMB owners need to focus on protecting their own livelihoods, as the consistent targets aren't really the governments or big businesses, but the SMBs themselves.

References:

"2020 Ransomware Statistics, Data, & Trends." *PurpleSec*, 20 Aug. 2020, purplesec.us/resources/cyber-security-statistics/ransomware/.

Allyn, Bobby. "22 Texas Towns Hit With Ransomware Attack In 'New Front' Of Cyberassault." *NPR*, NPR, 20 Aug. 2019, www.npr.org/2019/08/20/752695554/23-texas-towns-hit-with-ransomware-attack-in-new-front-of-cyberassault.

Duncan, Ian, and Colin Campbell. "Baltimore City Government Computer Network Hit by Ransomware Attack." *Baltimoresun.com*, Baltimore Sun, 30 June 2019, www.baltimoresun.com/politics/bs-md-ci-it-outage-20190507-story.html.

---

[11] "2020 Ransomware Statistics, Data, & Trends." *PurpleSec*, 20 Aug. 2020, purplesec.us/resources/cyber-security-statistics/ransomware/.
[12] IBID

"Information on the Capital One Cyber Incident." *2019 Capital One Cyber Incident | What Happened | Capital One*, 23 Sept. 2019, www.capitalone.com/facts2019/.

McCoy, Kevin. "Target to Pay $18.5M for 2013 Data Breach That Affected 41 Million Consumers." *USA Today*, Gannett Satellite Information Network, 23 May 2017, www.usatoday.com/story/money/2017/05/23/target-pay-185m-2013-data-breach-affected-consumers/102063932/.

"The Cost of Ransomware Attacks." *Nationwide*, Aug. 2020, www.nationwide.com/cps/cic/blog/cost-of-ransomware-attacks.html.

"Ransomware." *FBI*, FBI, 3 Apr. 2020, www.fbi.gov/scams-and-safety/common-scams-and-crimes/ransomware.

"What Is Business Continuity and Disaster Recovery (BCDR)? - Definition from Techopedia." *Techopedia.com*, 17 Jan. 2017, www.techopedia.com/definition/13767/business-continuity-and-disaster-recovery-bcdr.

About the Author

Mike Bloomfield is the President of Tekie Geek, a Managed Service Provider (MSP) headquartered in Staten Island, NY. Mike is seen as an IT expert throughout the IT community and is regularly published in numerous IT publications including Tech Decisions, ChannelPro Magazine, Channel Executive, and others. In 2020, Mike was also recognized as an Amazon bestselling author for his book, Hack Proof Your Business, Volume 2.

Tekie Geek is an award-winning MSP, with its core services being Managed IT Services, Business Continuity, Cloud Computing, and Unified Communication. With these core services, Tekie Geek is able to cure your IT ailments, properly protect your business from the rising IT threats, and detect issues before they even arise, giving you peace of mind and helping you to sleep better at night. They do this while maintaining their core company values of Clients, Culture, and Community.

Mike has had a passion for technology since an early age and has continued to push forward to ensure that he is always at the forefront of all technological advances. Before being President Geek of Tekie Geek, Mike has held such positions as IT/Research and Development Director and Manager of Product Engineering in the corporate world.

When Mike isn't focusing on his business, he's spending time with his beautiful wife, Nicole, and daughters, Audriana and Alexis. Mike gives the credit to his family for giving him the drive to keep going strong every day. He's a true geek at heart and it becomes obvious when you start to talk Marvel or Star Wars movies with him. It also becomes obvious when you see his vast collection of collectible figures and statues throughout the Tekie Geek office.

Business Awards

Staten Island Chamber of Commerce Lou Miller Award
SIEDC 20 Under 40 Award
SIEDC Top 31 Businesses in Staten Island
SIEDC Top 31 Fastest Growing Businesses in Staten Island
Star Network King of Staten Island

Star Network Power Duo of Staten Island
Star Network Stars Under 40
Channel Futures MSP 501

Organizations

Board of Directors, Meals on Wheels of Staten
Island
Board of Directors, Treasurer, Staten Island
Business Outreach Center
Board of Directors, Staten Island Board of Realtors
Board of Directors, Co-Chair, South Shore BID
Board of Directors, The Executive Club of Staten
Island
Advisory Board, MailProtector
Advisory Board, CryptoStopper

Contact Details

To schedule a consultation for your Business IT
needs, please get in touch with us:

Website: https://www.tekiegeek.com

Client Testimonial Videos:
https://love.tekiegeek.com

Email: sales@tekiegeek.com

Facebook: https://facebook.com/tekiegeek

Phone: (347) 830-7322

Made in the USA
Middletown, DE
01 December 2020